BUSY MUM'S COOKBOOK

WENDY CRAIG

Busy Mum's Cookbook

HAMLYN

London . New York . Sydney . Toronto

Published by The Hamlyn Publishing Group Limited
London . New York . Sydney . Toronto
Astronaut House, Feltham, Middlesex, England
© Copyright The Hamlyn Publishing Group Limited 1983

ISBN 0 600 32345 5

Illustrations by Robin Lawrie
Photography by David Johnson
Styling by Kit Johnson
Front cover photograph by James Jackson

Filmset in England by Photocomp Limited, Birmingham
Printed in Italy

The publishers would like to thank the following
for their kindness in providing items used
in the photography for this book:
Carpetcraft (Southern), St. Margaret's Road, East Twickenham
Perrings
The Reject Shop

Contents

Useful Facts and Figures

Notes on metrication

In this book quantities are given in metric and Imperial measures. Exact conversion from Imperial to metric measures does not usually give very convenient working quantities and so the metric measures have been rounded off into units of 25 grams. The table below shows the recommended equivalents.

Ounces	Approx g to nearest whole figure	Recommended conversion to nearest unit of 25	Ounces	Approx g to nearest whole figure	Recommended conversion to nearest unit of 25
1	28	25	11	312	300
2	57	50	12	340	350
3	85	75	13	368	375
4	113	100	14	396	400
5	142	150	15	425	425
6	170	175	16 (1 lb)	454	450
7	198	200	17	482	475
8	227	225	18	510	500
9	255	250	19	539	550
10	283	275	20 (1¼ lb)	567	575

Note: When converting quantities over 20 oz first add the appropriate figures in the centre column, then adjust to the nearest unit of 25. As a general guide, 1 kg (1000 g) equals 2·2 lb or about 2 lb 3 oz. This method of conversion gives good results in nearly all cases, although in certain pastry and cake recipes a more accurate conversion is necessary to produce a balanced recipe.

Liquid measures. The millilitre has been used in this book and the following table gives a few examples.

Imperial	Approx ml to nearest whole figure	Recommended ml	Imperial	Approx ml to nearest whole figure	Recommended ml
¼ pint	142	150 ml	1 pint	567	600 ml
½ pint	283	300 ml	1½ pints	851	900 ml
¾ pint	425	450 ml	1¾ pints	992	1000 ml (1 litre)

Spoon measures. All spoon measures given in this book are level unless otherwise stated.

Can sizes. At present, cans are marked with the exact (usually to the nearest whole number) metric equivalent of the Imperial weight of the contents, so we have followed this practice when giving can sizes.

Oven temperatures

The table below gives recommended equivalents.

	°C	°F	Gas Mark		°C	°F	Gas Mark
Very cool	110	225	$\frac{1}{4}$	Moderately	190	375	5
	120	250	$\frac{1}{2}$	hot	200	400	6
Cool	140	275	1	Hot	220	425	7
	150	300	2		230	450	8
Moderate	160	325	3	Very hot	240	475	9
	180	350	4				

Note: When making any of the recipes in this book, only follow one set of measures as they are not interchangeable.

Introduction

I know what it's like to be a busy mum. I've been one, and now I'm a busy grand-mum. This doesn't mean that currently I'm without gaping mouths to feed. Like baby birds in a nest, my family often visit me, and there is my husband (bless him for being so undemanding about food). However, my domestic situation has eased a lot since the boys left home. Frankly, I could have done with this book myself years ago when my sons were small, and I was finally driven to making the vital decision that I could not go on cooking a different dish for each person in the family at every main meal. I learned the rudiments of cooking from my mother, but I didn't take a real interest in it until I had my own family to feed. Somehow, my husband and sons have survived my culinary attempts, and my two lovely grand-daughters enjoy my Sunday lunches and teas, so I thought it might be useful to pass on what I'd learned to other busy mums.

Journalists have asked me many times: 'As an actress, mother and housewife, how do you manage to juggle with these rôles and keep them successfully spinning in the air?' The answer is, I don't . . . all the time. I just try to. Mine was not a large family – I only had two sons – but their eating habits were totally different. The elder one found the whole idea of eating totally boring. He wanted the sort of food that would slip down easily and un-noticed, preferably from a spoon. His brother, three-and-a-half years younger, had a hearty, but fairly eccentric appetite. For instance, he'd come in from school, throw his satchel in the corner, and wolf down a box of chocolate cup cakes in a matter of seconds. Why did I tolerate this hedonistic whim? I was weak, I suppose. He had to eat something before he started his homework, and it was obvious that the cakes satisfied his need for something to stimulate energy, as well as catering for a spot of self-indulgence after a tough day in the classroom. The anticipation of cup cakes made for a peaceful and rewarding return to the nest, and as long as I remembered to buy five boxes every Monday, it in no way affected the rest of the family. As expected, he eventually tired of them, and began to eat the same sort of teatime meal as the rest of us. That is, as long as it didn't include pastry. He was rather a nervous child, prone to anxieties, and one of the fears that haunted him was 'feeling sick'. He would only touch what he classed a 'safe food', and for him, pastry definitely didn't belong in that category. It had once caused him a tummy upset, and nothing would persuade him to risk it again. Hence, no pies, scones, tarts, nor anything which even vaguely resembled pastry could he tolerate within eyeshot.

Fads and Fancies

I am of the firm opinion that children are very canny about what makes them feel ill, and I don't think they should be forced into eating anything which really worries them. After all, most adults would be wary of eating oysters, if on a previous occasion they had suffered because of them. Although our elder son didn't care much about the content of his meals, it took much patience and gentle persuasion to get him to concentrate on chewing and swallowing. He'd just pack his cheeks full like a hamster and sit there with an angelic beam. When he was a tot I'd spend ages coaxing him . . . a spoonful of food being chuff-chuffed into his mouth like a train into a tunnel. It wasn't that he didn't like eating . . . he just could not be bothered. Although I don't have to play trains to get him to eat, perhaps the same could be said of my husband. He has always settled for anything on offer, which often is just as well. Perhaps the fact that he was in the army for years as a boy soldier case-hardened his stomach, but whatever the reason, I'm grateful.

On the other hand, the same cannot be said of my attitude to food. I was used to eating in restaurants before I married. My tastes were varied and exotic, I loved fancy foods from various countries, and as a wife I made gallant attempts to cook them myself. The one thing that used to exasperate my husband was watching me work myself up into a frenzy trying to cope with the individual desires of the children at the same time as preparing a complicated main meal to satisfy my own epicurean yearnings. 'What a lot of trouble you go to to get heartburn,' he'd growl.

Busy Actress *v* Busy Mum

My combined life of acting and running a home was fairly chaotic. I'd come rushing home from rehearsals after having shopped in the lunch hour for the various ingredients that might tickle the family's taste buds. Then the frantic mixed meal preparation, stirring two pans at once whilst figuratively mashing potatoes with my feet, while trying to ignore the bewildered looks of a family fearing for my blood pressure and my sanity. I think the final crunch came one day when I dashed home armed to the teeth with bulging plastic carrier bags, to find a note on the table stating : 'Sit down and relax, darling. I've taken them out to a Chinese restaurant for a peaceful meal.' It makes me smile now, but at the time I felt hurt . . . I was a failure. Then, as I sank into the sofa it dawned on me what absolute sense my spouse's message made. Not that we should always eat in a Chinese restaurant, but that we should all eat a dish which as far as possible we all liked, that it should be from the same cooking pot.

Thereupon, I decided to calmly work out a plan. I drew up a list of individual likes and dislikes and worked out a common denominator of sorts. This seemed to consist of chips, tripe and onions, fish fingers, baked beans, steak au poivre, cup cakes and Instant Whip: nutritious, but hardly inspiring – in fact, limiting, to say the least. No doubt about it, I'd have to broaden the family's gastronomic outlook if my scheme was going to work, and I'd have to stick very firmly to my resolution, because there would be considerable opposition on the junior front. Old habits die hard.

Surprisingly, once I'd made my decision, it wasn't as hard to carry through as I'd imagined. It did, however, take a bit of thought and planning ahead. Minced beef figured strongly in the early days. It made cottage pies, meat balls in tomato sauce, spaghetti bolognese, and home-made hamburgers. I suppose I was cheating a little, because these were the few old favourites I could rely upon. The difficult part was introducing new dishes and remaining absolutely steadfast in my resolve not to yield to any whining for specialised tastes. Either they ate what I gave them or they went hungry. I was determined not to force them. Nothing makes a child clamp his jaws together more tightly than being forced. I often felt dreadfully hard as I cleared away almost full plates and said, 'No, you can't have chips instead.'

Eventually, however, the idea sank in, and they began to eat what they were given with, albeit, resignation at first, and later with acceptance. Then I became fractionally more adventurous. Tinned salmon and tuna fish made excellent fish pies and home-made fish cakes. Eggs, too, were versatile and cheap. One big Spanish omelette cut up into portions went down a treat. Eggs baked on a bed of ham with a little double cream poured over them really got their gastric juices going. Corned beef made into a hash or sliced and fried in batter was well received. Of course, occasionally I had to compromise, because the spectre of the hated pastry still lurked. Rather than do the others out of steak and kidney pie, I baked the pastry (frozen flaky) separately and gave it only to those who wanted it. Success begat success and I began to be even more inventive. Campbells condensed soups did wonders to add flavour. For instance, a can of their vegetable soup added to minced lamb and onions in a cottage pie made it truly delicious, as did cream of chicken over a chicken casserole mixed in with the stock. French mustard spread over herrings before I baked them was a tasty trick, and a sprinkling of Worcester sauce over almost anything savoury added extra bite.

Family Favourites

It sounds a little puritanical, but I tried to keep chips down to a minimum, and therefore they became a Saturday lunchtime treat. Since childhood I've always felt that Saturday was a particularly happy sort of day, and chips enhanced that illusion. Incidentally, my children have always loved bottled tomato sauce. I saw no reason why they shouldn't continue to have it if they wished, since I love it, too. Fresh vegetables I either cooked in a casserole with the meat, or served separately with (compromising again) tinned tomatoes, baked beans, frozen peas or the newly discovered favourite, tinned or frozen

sweet corn tossed in butter and sprinkled with pepper. The preparation, and consequently the eating, of main meals, became gradually calmer. I admit I felt a little guilty when lack of time pushed me into a corner, and I offered up convenience foods, such as frozen beefburgers, fish fingers or bangers, until it was pointed out to me by a sensible district nurse, that these products were actually high in nutritional value, and that when I was under work pressure there was absolutely no reason at all to get myself into a state of exhaustion trying to prepare *everything* myself.

My husband, who in moments of bonhomie is not inclined to do things by halves, went out one day and bought me an enormous fridge. It was large enough for a restaurant, and had stamped across its back 'TROPICAL'. It was so big it stood in the middle of the kitchen like a jumbo jet waiting for take-off. I didn't want to hurt his feelings, but it was terribly in the way. Once again, all or nothing at all, he whipped the door off the broom cupboard, pushed the fridge into the recess and, voila! I had a marvellous cold pantry (I put the brooms under the stairs). I still have that fridge today: it holds all my tinned fruit, meat and fish, plus salads, cold joints, dog meat, everything . . . just like a big cold larder.

Fired with success, he next bought me a Kenwood mixer, complete with all the gadgets, followed by a freezer. So much technical aid went straight to my head. In next to no time I was making ice cream, freezing home-grown vegetables and becoming a bore boasting of all this endeavour to my friends. Oh, the delight of our own runner beans for a December Sunday lunch! The freezer, of course, meant I could save myself work by cooking in bulk. For instance, if I made a spaghetti sauce, I'd make double the amount and keep half of it to reheat another day. The same went for fish or cottage pies. I'd make two and freeze one in a foil dish. With storage like this I no longer needed to shop every day, either. I'd make a big list and shop for most of the things I'd need early in the week when the prices were lower. Of, if rehearsal time didn't allow for that, I'd do a big 'shop' at one of the late-night supermarkets. This meant I didn't have to go racing round in my lunch hour practically fainting from hunger at the sight of the delicatessen counter. I could actually go to the studio canteen and have a bite with my friends, and a sit down.

Cooking Under Pressure

I think my final graduation from bewildered beginner to reasonably organised family caterer took place when I embarked on a pressure cooker. There is no question about it, they are an amazing help. When you consider you can cook a chicken casserole from start to finish in half an hour, potatoes in five minutes, a pot roast, with vegetables, in less than an hour, there can be no argument that they are a busy mum's life saver. When I first experimented with mine I was extremely nervous. I was convinced it would explode, and I kept edging fearfully behind the kitchen door. Of course, this was nonsense. Used properly, they are perfectly safe, and probably the most useful cooking gadget one could possess.

This book is not, of course, the answer to all your family's eating problems, but it may help iron out quite a lot of them, and give you a few ideas. Children's eating habits don't really change that much as they grow into adulthood. I find my elder son is still a very slow and reluctant eater, and his daughters now shout, 'Hurry up, Daddy, Granny wants to give us pudding!' As for his brother . . . well, I still can't imagine him marrying a pastry cook.

What about Breakfast?

For busy mums, breakfast is probably the worst time of the day: late-for-school children, lost-in-the-bathroom children, the scramble for satchels, coats and gloves, not to mention the equally urgent need to get a busy dad fed and on his way, all these tend to wear away the cornflake-ad image of the happy family breakfasting blissfully together. More perhaps than at any other meal of the day, there will be strong disagreement as to what exactly, or how much, each member of the family wants to eat. All mothers know that it is important for young children, who go to bed early, to have breakfast; missing it out leaves too long a gap between meals, not a good thing for them or their schoolwork. But, happily, it doesn't really matter what kind of breakfast they have – the simplest, uncooked things are just as good as the cooked. Today's breakfast favourites are easy to store, so there is no problem about providing a good selection to choose from: milk or fruit juice are of course excellent drinks, here or at any time, a selection of cereals, or just toast, are perfectly good breakfast fodder that take only a moment to put on the table and to eat. Muesli is probably the best form of instant breakfast of this kind, and the most interesting, so here is a recipe for a good mix that can be prepared ahead in a sizeable quantity and stored.

Mum's Muesli

8 tablespoons honey
6 tablespoons oil
1 tablespoon vanilla essence
450 g / 1 lb medium oat flakes
175 g / 6 oz sesame seeds
100 g / 4 oz desiccated coconut
50 g / 2 oz wheatgerm
100 g / 4 oz dried apricots, coarsely chopped

Set the oven at moderate (180 C, 350 F, gas 4). Stir the honey, oil and vanilla essence together in a pan and heat gently. Add all the remaining ingredients and mix as thoroughly as possible so that everything is coated in the honey mixture.

Transfer the cereal to a large, shallow baking tin or dish and bake it in the oven for 15 to 20 minutes or until lightly browned. Check frequently to make sure it does not stick or burn and stir it every 5 minutes.

Remove the cereal from the oven, allow to cool and transfer it to a storage jar.

Serve this high-protein, maximum-crunch cereal with milk. Fresh fruit should be very popular with it too, and finishes it off perfectly: try grated crispy apple, sliced banana or pear; segmented clementines are perhaps most tempting of all, so make the most of their short season.

In winter, a cooked breakfast is always an encouraging start to the day, and, fortunately, here too the simplest, quickest ideas are likely to be the popular ones as well. Scrambled egg is a cinch – especially if you provide yourself with a non-stick pan to cut out that dreaded washing up problem. Topped with bacon and bedded on toast, it can't be bettered for the children and causes the minimum stress to mum.

But what about the child who won't eat in the morning, *at all?* Well, it's not worth turning breakfast-time into a battleground over: that does no good to anyone at the time, and can blight the rest of the day for all involved. The best thing you can do is to pack a basic-breakfast-kit – say, an apple, a couple of biscuits or a muesli bar, plus a covered cup or a small carton of milk – into the satchel for him or her to help themselves to at the mid-morning break.

About Nutrition

For the mum of any family – and most of all to those of us busy outside the home as well – there is an implied accusation in the very word 'nutrition'. Today, in the face of the vast choice of processed foods on the supermarket shelf it carries a distinct threat: suggesting that all this convenience food can't be good for us, that we aren't getting enough of the 'right', i.e. the 'nutritious', things . . . that fish fingers might indeed be the death of us. The most important – and, the most heartening – thing to remember about this highly emotional subject is that most of our fears are groundless: it really is far easier than you think to provide a fair balance of good yet easily prepared meals. It is not essential either to weigh and measure gram by gram or meal by meal, what we propose to give the family to eat, and devise each individual dish accordingly. Not even the most demented nutritionist could live with such a routine (and most decidedly no family could!).

What we can do, if we are beginners at family meal making, or feel that we are not including enough of the right things in their diet, is to look at what we give them week by week, and adjust accordingly. The simplest way of making sure we are providing the essentials is to vary our meals, to base some on meat, others on fish, eggs, cheese, vegetables or cereals. If you think about it, in day-to-day cooking this is pretty likely to happen anyway, if only because of the cries of protest a monotonous diet brings from our helpless offspring.

However, as a basic, reassuring checklist, opposite is a table of the major nutrients in each of six groups of foods.

Table of healthy eating

	Food	How often / How much	What it gives
Group 1	Lean meat, fish and poultry, eggs	Eat up to once a day Eat frequently Eat up to 7 a week	Proteins, fats, B group vitamins, iron
Group 2	Skimmed milk, cottage cheese, low fat yogurt	Eat two portions daily	Calcium, proteins, Vitamins A and D, fats
Group 3	Fruits and vegetables	Eat at least three good portions daily	Starches (complex carbohydrates) Vitamin C, dietary fibre
Group 4	Wholemeal cereals, bread, pasta, rice	Eat at least three portions daily	Starches, proteins, B group vitamins, iron, calcium, dietary fibre
Group 5	Butter, margarine	Eat some, but not more than 15-25 g / $\frac{1}{2}$-1 oz daily	Fats, Vitamins A and D
Group 6	Oils, lard, cream, sugar	Eat as little as you can, unless you are extremely active	Fats, sugars (simple carbohydrates)

The nutrients listed for each group are only a small sample of the total contained, but they are the major ones. As long, therefore, as we eat foods from each of the first five groups we are almost certain to be getting not just the essentials mentioned here, but all the others as well. As a rough guide, two portions (i.e. normal, average helpings) of foods from each of groups 1 and 2 every day or 3 from each of groups 3 and 4 should provide enough of all nutrients. But, as this may not give very active members of the family sufficient energy, additional foods from any of the groups, including group 6 which contains fat and sugar rather than proteins, vitamins or minerals, may be eaten. Fats and sugars are particularly good providers of energy (calories); but if any member of your family has a weight problem these foods must be the first to be restricted.

Drawing up a good eating plan

Advising any mum to produce two portions from groups 1 and 2 and three from groups 3 and 4 in the table for every member of the family every day is a counsel of perfection – all very well if you have time and opportunity to prepare three meals a day. But today this is likely to be an impossibility. So what to do? Well, the first thing is to relax and reassure yourself – if you didn't know it already – that many convenience foods are good news all round, price-wise, time-wise *and* nutrition-wise. As long as you choose sensibly, (which means a bit of initial shopping around, trying out and label-watching) there is no doubt that the nutritional value of those time-saving meals can be every bit as good as those grown, picked and prepared with your own hands. Sandwiches, beefburgers, baked beans on toast, pizza, ice cream, and the all-time favourite fish fingers are equally justifiable: they're not just top of the popularity poll, they're good value too, in every sense. Just remember two things: (a) your table of food groups, in relation to (b) the foods your children are liable to get at school. Crisps, squashes and quick snacks are likely to be low in vitamins and minerals and heavy on calories, so make sure that what you give them at home is biased in the opposite direction. Then all should be well.

How much does your child need?

Just like adults, children have wildly different appetites and needs when it comes to food. Some are constantly hungry and eat like horses at every meal, others pick and choose more like wasting jockeys. Try not to let such things worry you – after all, if he or she generally seems healthy then all is probably well. Guidelines for age/height/weight are of only limited use since some children do most of their growing very young, while others leave it until well into their teens. On the whole a child eats as much as he needs; a few days off food in general or a passion for one particular food to the seeming exclusion of other old favourites isn't serious. If you have been building up good eating habits (and this means taking note of the table on page 15) then your children are eating well enough most of the time to have acquired substantial reserves of vitamins, minerals, proteins and even some energy, and can come to no harm if one of the groups is not eaten as often as is ideal, for days, or even a week or two.

Main Meals

I have found that one of the biggest difficulties in catering for a family is actually getting everyone to stop whatever activity they happen to be doing and assemble themselves around the table. Children become so engrossed in pastimes that they usually have to be almost physically dragged away from them, and husbands are almost as bad.

I've found that the best way is to give them a warning yell that the meal is imminent about ten minutes before you're going to serve it up. This gives time for a second or third and final call, which can be accompanied by banging a wooden spoon on a pan, or if you live in that sort of style, sounding a gong. They will then have time to put away whatever they're using and wash their hands. It's a good idea to get members of the family to take turns in laying the table and putting the plates to warm.

Table manners need not be Victorian, but you will not do yourself or them any favours by allowing them to do just as they please. Bad-mannered children are not popular when they go visiting and they have a hard time when faced with school dinners. Tensions are bound to arise occasionally, especially if father is exhausted after a hard day's work, and the children are playing up, but develop a sense of humour about it, if you can. Clearing the table and washing up should be shared by those capable of helping. Mothers are not slaves, and if they've prepared the meal, then it's not fair to expect them to wash up too.

QUICK CASSEROLES

I'm a great fan of those cans of cook-in-sauces that are just poured over meat and vegetables and simmered slowly in the oven. Very quickly and easily, you can create a variety of interesting, nourishing casseroles. The selection below should give you a few ideas on how effortlessly you can make the most of many of the cheaper cuts of meat. Here is where a pressure cooker comes into its own.

Braised Steak

2 tablespoons vegetable oil
450 g / 1 lb braising steak cut into 4 pieces
1 (227-g / 8-oz) packet frozen casserole vegetables
100 g / 4 oz button mushrooms
1 (376-g / 13¼-oz) can red wine cook-in-sauce

Set the oven at moderate, 180 C, 350 F, gas 4. Heat the oil in a large flameproof casserole on top of the stove. When the oil is very hot add the meat, two pieces at a time, and quickly brown on both sides. Remove onto a plate.

Turn the heat down low and add the frozen vegetables to the casserole. Stir through, then cook for 5 minutes stirring occasionally. Rinse the mushrooms and stir these into the other vegetables. Add the browned meat and pour over the red wine sauce. Cover the casserole and place in the heated oven for 1½ hours, stirring occasionally. Serve with mashed potatoes or rice. SERVES 4.

It is also worth looking at condensed soups. A can poured over browned meat – chops, cubed braising steak, or liver, chicken pieces, and simmered slowly in the oven, cuts out making a sauce. Add fresh or frozen vegetables (onions, carrots, leeks, parsnips, beans, peas, or tomatoes) and flavourings (herbs, spices, garlic) to taste for a superb flavour.

Try also poaching fish steaks in cream of smoked salmon or crab bisque condensed soups.

Mighty Meatball Casserole

Another idea is to simmer meatballs in a cook-in-sauce. Use any flavour sauce (or condensed soup) you like – mushroom and red wine, curry and goulash are particularly good.

1 tablespoon oil
1 small onion, chopped
450 g / 1 lb lean minced beef
50 g / 2 oz fresh brown breadcrumbs
1 egg, beaten
salt, pepper and mustard powder to taste
1 tablespoon tomato ketchup
1 clove garlic, crushed (optional)
1 tablespoon flour
oil for frying
1 (376-g / 13·25-oz) can cook-in-sauce

Set the oven at 190 C, 375 F, gas 5. Heat the oil in a frying pan, add the onion and fry until soft. Meanwhile, mix the minced beef with the breadcrumbs, egg, seasonings, ketchup and garlic, if using. Stir in the cooked onion. Divide the mixture into 12, and shape into balls. Roll in the flour. Heat a little oil in the frying pan and quickly brown the meatballs, in several batches. Drain well. Place in an ovenproof casserole or dish and pour over the sauce. Cover and cook in the heated oven for 30 to 40 minutes. Serves 4.

Serve with spaghetti or macaroni and a salad.

Two little tips. For small children, who might find the flavour of cook-in-sauces a bit strong as they are, I dilute them with half a tin of water. Also, for me, the tomato and onion version is all the better for the addition of a few tablespoons of extra (tinned) tomato sauce, and the same of lemon juice.

If you've put too much salt in a casserole, add a little cream or milk. You can also try cooking some potatoes in it, even for 10 minutes (they absorb salt).

Weekend Chicken

Illustrated on page 33

4 chicken portions
1 (283-g / 10-oz) can sweetcorn, drained
1 (376-g / 13½-oz) can tomato and onion cook-in-sauce

Set the oven at moderate, 180 C, 350 F, gas 4. Put the chicken and sweetcorn in an ovenproof casserole, pour over the sauce and stir to mix the ingredients.

Cover and cook in the heated oven for 1½ hours, stirring from time to time.

Serve with spaghetti, noodles or Sticky Rice (page 107). SERVES 4.

Chinese Chicken

Illustrated on pages 44-5

3 tablespoons vegetable oil
2 cloves garlic, crushed
2·5-cm / 1-in piece fresh root ginger, peeled and chopped
1 (437-g / 15-oz) can pineapple chunks in natural juice
2 teaspoons cornflour
1 tablespoon sherry
½ teaspoon salt
4 chicken breasts, cut into cubes
spring onions (optional garnish)

Heat the oil in a wok or frying pan. Add the garlic and ginger and fry over low heat. Drain the juice from the pineapple and mix it with the cornflour, sherry and salt. Add the chicken to the frying pan and stir fry over high heat. When the meat has turned white (about 3 minutes) add the cornflour / juice mixture and the pineapple. Stir until the mixture boils. Simmer for 1 minute, taste for seasoning. Serve with boiled rice. If liked, garnish with spring onions. SERVES 4.

Chicken Pie

2 (170-g /6-oz) packs frozen chicken supremes, thawed
3 tablespoons cream or top of the milk
2 stalks celery, sliced
1 tablespoon chopped parsley
1 (85-g /3-oz) sheet frozen puff pastry
beaten egg to glaze

Set the oven at 200 C, 400 F, gas 6.

Mix together the thawed chicken supremes, cream, celery and parsley. Spoon into a 20-cm /8-in oval ovenproof pie dish. Thaw the pastry at room temperature for 10 minutes, then roll out to an oblong 23 cm /9 in long and 18 cm /7½ in wide. Cut a strip 1 cm /½ in wide from the outer edges of the pastry oblong. Brush the rim of the pie dish with beaten egg and press the pastry strip onto the rim, then brush the strip with beaten egg and carefully cover the dish with pastry. Trim off the excess with a sharp knife. Using a fork, press the pastry in firmly to seal. Flute the edges and use any pastry trimmings to decorate the pie, if wished. Brush the pie with beaten egg. Place on a baking sheet and bake in the heated oven for 20 minutes till golden brown. SERVES 4 to 6.

Variations

Replace 1 (170-g /6-oz) pack chicken supremes with a 198-g /7-oz can sweetcorn, or 100-g /4-oz packet frozen peas, thawed, or 175 g /6 oz fresh mushrooms, sliced.

Devilled Chicken

25 g / 1 oz butter
250 g / 8 oz button mushrooms
350 g / 12 oz cooked chicken, diced
300 ml / ½ pint wholemilk yogurt
2 teaspoons cornflour
3 tablespoons tomato ketchup
2 teaspoons Worcestershire sauce
½ teaspoon mustard
1-2 drops tabasco sauce (optional)
salt and pepper to taste

Set the oven at 250 C, 400 F, gas 6. Melt the butter in a frying pan and fry the mushrooms until golden. Drain the cooked mushrooms in a colander set over a plate and place them in an ovenproof baking dish or soufflé dish with the diced chicken. Mix the yogurt with the cornflour until smooth, then mix in the ketchup, Worcestershire sauce, mustard, tabasco (if using) and season to taste with salt and pepper. Pour over the mushroom and chicken mixture and bake in the heated oven for 15 minutes. SERVES 4.

This dish makes a quick and easy meal served with rice and peas or broccoli. For a first course or small supper dish, make a half quantity and bake in 4 individual ramekins for 10 minutes.

Scallopini

Illustrated on page 33

275 g / 10 oz spaghetti
4 thin escalopes of pork, veal or turkey
4 tablespoons flour
1 egg, beaten
100 g / 4 oz fresh breadcrumbs
25 g / 1 oz grated parmesan cheese
oil for frying
1 (310-g / 10·9-oz) jar Italian or Napoletana tomato sauce
25 g / 1 oz butter
salt and pepper to taste

Cook the spaghetti in boiling salted water until tender, about 15 minutes. Meanwhile, prepare the scallopini. If necessary, lightly beat out the escalopes to flatten them, using a meat hammer or rolling pin dipped in cold water. Dip the escalopes in flour, then in beaten egg. Mix the breadcrumbs with the parmesan and use to coat the escalopes, pressing the crumbs onto the meat.

Heat a little oil in a large frying pan and fry the escalopes until brown and crisp, about 2 minutes each side. It may be necessary to cook the escalopes in two batches. Keep them warm whilst draining the spaghetti and heating the tomato sauce. Toss the spaghetti with the butter and a little salt and pepper. Serve the escalopes on a bed of spaghetti. Spoon a little of the sauce over the escalopes, and serve the rest separately. SERVES 4.

Not-just-for-spaghetti Sauce

Make a large quantity of this and freeze it in useful (say, 4-serving) portions. It is one of the most versatile recipes you can spend time on, because, as you will see from the ideas below, it can make many a good and satisfying meal.

2 tablespoons oil
2 large onions, sliced
450 g / 1 lb lean minced beef
1½ tablespoons flour
4 tablespoons tomato purée
1 (396-g / 14-oz) can chopped tomatoes
1-2 cloves garlic (optional or to taste)
fresh or dried basil, to taste
salt and pepper to taste

Heat the oil in a large saucepan, add the onion and cook gently until soft and transparent, about 15 minutes. Push to one side and turn up the heat. Add the meat and cook, stirring to break up any lumps, until browned. Stir in the flour, tomato purée, tomatoes, garlic if using, basil and a little salt and pepper. Cover and simmer gently for 30 minutes. Taste and adjust the seasoning if necessary. Serve with spaghetti, or as suggested below. SERVES 6.

Shepherd's Pie

Omit the garlic and basil and replace the tomato purée with tomato ketchup. Add 1 tablespoon Worcestershire sauce. Peel 675 g / 1½ lb potatoes. Boil until tender, drain and mash until smooth. Beat in 25 g / 1 oz butter and 150 ml / ¼ pint hot milk and salt and pepper to taste.

Spoon the meat sauce into an ovenproof baking dish and top with the mashed potatoes, smoothing them to make an even layer. If wished, sprinkle with a little grated cheese or decorate with a few slices of tomato.

Bake in an oven preheated to 190 C, 375 F, gas 5 for 25 minutes until bubbling. SERVES 4 to 6.

Goulash

Omit the basil. Add 2 tablespoons of mild paprika to the saucepan and fry with the meat. Stir in 3 tablespoons soured cream or yogurt just before serving with noodles or rice.

Chilli beans

Omit the basil. Add chilli powder to taste to the saucepan with the meat. Drain a 425-g/15-oz can red kidney beans and stir in with the canned tomatoes.

Curry Crumble

Illustrated on pages 44-5

Omit the basil and the tomato purée. Add curry powder to taste to the saucepan with the meat. Simmer for about 15 minutes. To make the crumble topping, mix together 100 g/4 oz flour, 100 g/4 oz porridge oats and a large pinch of salt. Rub in 125 g/5 oz butter, stir 1 tablespoon mango chutney and 1 tablespoon desiccated coconut into the meat mixture. Spoon into an ovenproof baking dish, top with the crumble and bake in an oven preheated to 180 C, 350 F, gas 4 for 20 minutes.

Toad-in-the-hole

175 g / 6 oz plain flour
½ teaspoon salt
3 eggs
200 ml / 7 fl oz milk
200 ml / 7 fl oz water
4 tablespoons cooking oil, lard or dripping
450 g / 1 lb sausages

Set the oven at moderately hot, 200 C, 400 F, gas 6.

First make the batter: sift the flour and salt into a mixing bowl, make a well in the centre, add the eggs and beat well, drawing in a little flour. Gradually beat in the milk and water and the remaining flour – this is much easier done with an electric whisk or a rotary hand whisk. Beat until the mixture is smooth. If a few lumps still remain, strain into a jug or another bowl.

Heat the oil, lard or dripping in 4 15-cm / 6-in pudding tins or a 25 × 23 cm / 10 × 9 in roasting tin in the oven for 5 minutes. Add the sausages and cook for 10 minutes until browned. Pour over the batter and return to the oven. Cook for a further 20 to 25 minutes until well-risen, crisp and golden brown. Remove from the pudding tins or roasting tin and serve immediately with gravy and peas or baked beans. SERVES 4.

Variation

Yorkshire Pudding. Follow the above recipe, for the batter only.

Incidentally, my children loved (and still do) having our left over Yorkshire Pudding as a sweet, with sugar and lemon or golden syrup and lemon.

Marmalade Pancake. Cook the batter as above, omitting the sausages. Spread the baked pudding with 6 tablespoons marmalade (or spread each individual pudding with 1½ tablespoons marmalade) or jam. Dust with a little icing sugar and return to the oven for a couple of minutes to heat through. Cut into wedges and serve immediately.

Beef Parcels

Illustrated on page 34

2 tablespoons oil
4 100-g/4-oz fresh or frozen beefburgers
2 tablespoons oil
2 sheets (half of a 340-g/12-oz packet frozen puff pastry sheets)
thawed
4 slices processed cheese
1 egg, beaten, to glaze

Set the oven at 200 C, 400 F, gas 6. Lightly grease a baking sheet. Heat the oil in a frying pan and quickly brown the beefburgers on both sides. Drain and leve to cool. Roll out each pastry sheet to an oblong 30 × 15 cm / 12 × 6 in. Cut each oblong in half, and place a beefburger in the middle of each pastry square. Cover with a slice of cheese. Brush the edges of the pastry with a little beaten egg, bring the pastry up over the filling and pinch the four corners together to seal. Brush with egg and transfer to the baking sheet. Bake in the heated oven for 20 minutes until crisp and golden. SERVES 4.

Loopy Liver

Illustrated on page 34

450 g / 1 lb lamb's liver
150 ml / $\frac{1}{4}$ pint milk
3 tablespoons oil
450 g / 1 lb onions, thinly sliced in rings
1 tablespoon flour
1 (310-g / 10·9-oz) jar Italian or Napoletana tomato sauce
150 ml / $\frac{1}{4}$ pint chicken or beef stock
350 g / 12 oz spaghetti or noodles
25 g / 1 oz butter
salt and pepper to taste

Trim any white ducts or membranes from the liver, then slice it into strips and soak in the milk for 10 minutes. Meanwhile, cook the spaghetti or noodles in boiling salted water, according to the directions on the packet. Drain the liver, and dry on paper towels. Heat half the oil in a frying pan and fry the liver, stirring constantly, for about 3 minutes until just tender. Remove from the pan and keep warm. Add the rest of the oil to the pan, then add the onions. Lower the heat and cook gently, stirring occasionally, until soft – about 10 minutes. Stir in the flour, then the tomato sauce and the stock. Bring to a boil, and simmer for 5 minutes. Add the liver to the pan, and remove from the heat. If the liver boils it will be tough. Add salt and pepper to taste. Drain the spaghetti or noodles when cooked, add the butter and a little salt and pepper and toss well. Transfer to a serving dish and spoon the liver and sauce on top, or add the liver and sauce to the spaghetti and toss well to mix. SERVES 4.

Corned Beef Fritters

The basic fritter batter below can be used to coat slices of spam, or fillets of fish as well as chicken or turkey steaks or escalopes. You can, too, coat chunks of banana or thick slices of apple in it and fry them for a quick pud. For a different 'starter' dip large mushrooms in batter and fry. Serve with tartare sauce. For easy 'Sweet and Sour Pork' dip 2/5-cm/1-in cubes of fillet of pork in fritter batter, for about 3 minutes, drain and serve with either the Sweet and Sour Sauce on page 38 or use a can of sweet and sour cook-in-sauce that has been heated in a saucepan. Serve with rice.

Basic Fritter Batter

100 g / 4 oz flour
generous pinch of salt
generous pinch of castor sugar
1 egg, separated
1 egg yolk
1 tablespoon oil
150 ml / $\frac{1}{4}$ pint milk

Mix together the flour, salt and sugar in a mixing bowl.

Make a well in the centre and add the 2 egg yolks, oil and milk. Gradually whisk the flour into the milk mixture to make a smooth batter. If possible, leave to stand for 30 minutes. Whisk the egg white until very stiff and fold into the batter. Use immediately.

Corned Beef Fritters

Basic Fritter Batter (see above)
1 (340-g / 12-oz) can corned beef
oil for deep frying

Chill the can of corned beef, overnight if possible. Open and slice the meat into 6 thick slices. Heat the oil to 190 C, 375 F. Coat the slices of meat in the batter and deep-fry for about 3 minutes, until golden and crispy. Drain on kitchen paper, and serve right away. SERVES 4.

SUNDAY LUNCH

Families may not be able to eat together as often as they did a generation or two ago, but I could always be sure that if there was one meal in the week my two boys would turn up for, this would be it. Its easy pace may not induce the exchange of views on important issues of the day that an old-fashioned father looked for, but it does for once give us time to sit down over a relaxed meal and catch up on what we've all been up to. From very early on too, children can enjoy the ritual of Sunday lunch making. The peeling of the roast potatoes, the preparing of the joint for the oven, the beating of the Yorkshire batter, and the final stirring of the gravy: quite small children can join in (and safely too!) with quite a few of these pleasant chores. It makes, too, one of the nicest ways I can think of for a child to begin to learn about good, simple food and how it is made. The following pages and the little section on vegetables between pages 47 and 51 will, I hope, give you quite a few ideas.

Stuffed Roast Chicken

Children like dark golden, crispy-skinned chicken, and this recipe is fool-proof

1·5 kg / 3 lb roasting chicken
1 large onion, quartered · 1 tablespoon plain flour
300 ml / $\frac{1}{2}$ pint chicken stock
STUFFING
100 g / 4 oz butter
1 small onion, finely chopped
100 g / 4 oz pork sausagemeat with herbs
100 g / 4 oz fresh wholemeal breadcrumbs
1 egg, beaten · salt and pepper

Set the oven at 220 C, 425 F, gas 7. First, make the stuffing. Melt 15 g / $\frac{1}{2}$ oz of the butter in a small pan, add the chopped onion and cook gently for 2 to 3 minutes until soft. Cool. Mix the sausagemeat with the crumbs, the cooled onion mixture, the egg and a little salt and pepper. Stuff the neck end of the chicken with this mixture (the neck end is the opposite end to the parson's nose). Put the quartered onion in the base of a roasting dish and place the chicken on top. Spread the remaining butter over the breast and legs of the chicken and sprinkle with salt and pepper. Roast in the heated oven for 1 hour, basting frequently, and adding half of the stock to the roasting dish after 45 minutes.

Remove the cooked chicken to a serving dish and keep warm. To make the gravy, put the roasting tin on top of the stove and stir over low heat to dislodge any meat juices that have stuck to the dish. Sprinkle in the flour, and cook, stirring constantly, for a few seconds. Add in the remaining stock and bring to a boil, stirring vigorously to prevent lumps. Taste for seasoning and add a little salt and pepper if necessary. Strain into a gravy boat. SERVES 4.

Variation

Before roasting, rub the chicken with a little butter, and sprinkle with plenty of fresh thyme, and add a little chopped parsley, chopped prunes or dried apricots to the stuffing.

A Guide to Roasting Times and Temperatures

Save work on oven-cleaning by wrapping the bird or joint in foil, but allow an extra 10 to 15 minutes' roasting time.

Chicken

Must be thoroughly defrosted. Rub with a little butter, and season with salt and pepper. Roast at 220 C, 425 F, gas 7 for 15 minutes per 450 g / 1 lb plus 15 minutes over. Serve with Bread Sauce (see page 36), roast potatoes and young peas.

Duck

Must be thoroughly defrosted.
  Prick the skin well to make it less greasy. Cooking time will be the same as for chicken.

Turkey

Again, defrost thoroughly at room temperature. Weigh the bird when stuffed – if it weighs up to 5·5 kg / 12 lb cook for 15 minutes per 450 g / 1 lb and 15 minutes over. For every 450 g / 1 lb over this weight add an extra 12 minutes. Start the turkey at 220 C, 425 F, gas 7 for 1 hour, then reduce the temperature to 200 C, 400 F, gas 6 for the remainder of the time. Protect the breast meat from drying out by laying 6 to 8 rashers streaky bacon over the top, and baste frequently. Serve with Bread Sauce (see page 36), roast potatoes, Brussels sprouts and chestnuts.

Beef

Sirloin, topside, rib of beef and fillet are good, if expensive cuts for roasting. Choose meat that has a little fat marbling to prevent it

Weekend Chicken (page 20), Yogurt Fool (page 57) and Scallopini (page 23).

becoming dry and tasteless. Rub a little salt and pepper into the joint and put a little dripping or oil into the roasting tin. For rare meat cook at 220 C, 425 F, gas 7 for 15 minutes per 450 g / 1 lb plus 15 minutes over, for well-done meat allow 20 minutes per 450 g / 1 lb and 20 minutes over. Serve with Yorkshire Pudding (page 26), and Horseradish Sauce (see overleaf). Apart from roast potatoes, other good vegetables would be carrots, courgettes or roast parsnips.

Lamb

Shoulder, leg, best end of neck and breast of lamb are the cuts to choose.

Prepare by scoring the meat in a criss-cross pattern. Rub the fat with oil, salt and pepper, and rosemary or thyme. You can too stick slivers of garlic into the meat. Roast at 220 C, 425 F, gas 7 for 20 minutes per 450 g / 1 lb plus 20 minutes over.

Serve with Mint Sauce (see overleaf) and / or redcurrant jelly. Young peas, new potatoes cooked with mint, or roast potatoes, and French beans are all excellent with lamb.

Pork

Choose loin, leg and spare ribs.

If the joint has not already been scored, do so yourself with a very sharp knife. Season the meat with salt and pepper, and to make sure you get the crispest possible crackling, rub it over with oil to begin with. Then, about 15 minutes before the end of the roasting time, you can slice it in one piece from the joint, put it in a separate pan, and return it to the top of the oven turned up high (220 C, 425 F, gas 7, or thereabouts). Roast the meat itself at 220 C, 425 F, gas 7 for 25 minutes per 450 g / 1 lb plus 20 minutes over. Serve with Apple Sauce (see overleaf). Roast potatoes, spinach or broccoli will go down very well with it too.

Loopy Liver (page 28) and a Beef Parcel (page 27).

Six Sauces for the Sunday Joint

Here is how to make a family-sized quantity of our favourite sauces, starting with the original, and for most of us still the best, sauce for roast meat:

Gravy

Pour off all but a couple of tablespoons of the juice from the roasting tin. Stand the tin over a low heat and stir in a good tablespoon of flour. Cook until the mixture turns a warm brown, stirring all the time so that the crisp pieces of meat from the pan are well mixed in. Gradually blend in about 300 ml / ½ pint stock or water and cook it, stirring, until the gravy comes to a boil and thickens. Simmer a couple of minutes more, season with salt and pepper, pour into a sauce boat and serve.

Bread Sauce

Peel a small onion and press 2 or 3 cloves into it. Put this, together with 300 ml / ½ pint milk and a few peppercorns and a piece of bay leaf, into a saucepan and bring slowly to a boil. Remove from the heat and leave to stand for 20 minutes or so. When ready to serve, strain the milk, return to the heat and stir in 50 g / 2 oz white breadcrumbs and a knob of butter. Stir until the sauce is hot, smooth and fairly thick, then season to taste and serve right away, with roast chicken or turkey.

Orange Sauce

This takes a little more time and trouble than the other sauces, but a rather more special bird like duck deserves it. Start by making the sauce base: melt 40 g / 1½ oz butter in a small pan, then add 1½ tablespoons flour and cook together for a few minutes over low heat. Add 450 ml / ¾ pint hot beef stock and simmer gently for about 30 minutes. While this is going on (and here comes the time-consuming bit) thinly peel the rind of 1 large orange and 1 lemon. Cut it into narrow strips and simmer in a pan of water for 3 minutes. Drain and add to the hot sauce. Otherwise, if you are too short of time to do this, simply grate the orange and lemon rinds and add them directly to the hot sauce. Whichever you do add also the juice of both fruits. Finally, add the roasting juices from the duck, reheat the sauce, check the flavour, adding a little sugar if necessary, and serve right away. If you wish, you can also peel away the pith of the orange, using a sharp knife, slice it, heat the slices in some of the sauce and garnish the duck with them.

Mint Sauce

Finely chop a handful of mint leaves and put them into a sauce bowl or jug. Pour over a few tablespoons of boiling water, a tablespoon of sugar and leave to get cold. Or, simplest of all, just whizz all of the ingredients together in a blender. Just before serving with your joint of lamb, add 3 tablespoons wine vinegar, stir well and adjust the flavourings to taste.

Apple Sauce

Peel and core 450 g/1 lb cooking apples and slice them into a saucepan. Add 3 tablespoons water and simmer, covered, until the apples are soft. Remove from the heat, beat to a pulp, and finish by beating in 15 g/$\frac{1}{2}$ oz butter and a tablespoon of sugar. Serve hot, right away, with roast pork.

Horseradish Sauce

Lightly whip 150 ml/$\frac{1}{4}$ pint double or whipping cream and fold into it 2-3 tablespoons grated fresh horseradish or proprietary creamed horseradish and the juice of half a lemon. Season with salt and a little sugar to taste. Perfect with roast beef.

Sweet and Sour Crispy Cod

Illustrated on pages 44-5

Either use a can of sweet and sour cook-in-sauce or use the quick homemade sauce recipe below.

225 g / 8 oz long grain American rice
450 ml / $\frac{3}{4}$ pint cold water
2 (200-g / 7-oz) packets frozen crispy cod fries
oil for frying
1 (376-g / 13$\frac{1}{4}$-oz) can sweet and sour cook-in-sauce

Wash the rice and put into a pan with the water – don't put in any salt. Bring to a boil and cook for about 5 minutes, until the water has evaporated to the same level as the rice. Cover the pan and cook on a very low flame for 10 minutes, without stirring or lifting the lid. Meanwhile, fry the cod fries in hot oil according to the instructions on the packet. Drain on absorbent paper. Heat the sweet and sour sauce very gently. Arrange the rice on a serving dish with the cod fries on top. Pour over the sauce and serve immediately. SERVES 4.

Homemade Sweet and Sour Sauce

1 can frozen concentrated orange juice
2 tablespoons soft brown sugar
3 tablespoons wine vinegar
2 tablespoons soy sauce
2 teaspoons cornflour mixed with 150 ml / $\frac{1}{4}$ pint cold water
salt and pepper to taste

Heat the orange juice, sugar, vinegar and soy sauce in a pan. Blend the cornflour with the water and stir into the sauce. Bring to a boil, stirring constantly to prevent lumps from forming. Season to taste with salt and pepper.

Salmon Saturday Special

Illustrated on page 43

2 (200-g / 7-oz) tins salmon
1 tablespoon lemon juice
20 g / $\frac{3}{4}$ oz butter
20 g / $\frac{3}{4}$ oz flour
250 ml / 8 fl oz milk
150 ml / $\frac{1}{4}$ pint single cream
salt and pepper to taste
1 egg, beaten
2 stalks celery, sliced
1 tablespoon chopped parsley or chives (optional)
100 g / 4 oz dried breadcrumbs

Set the oven at 180 C, 350 F, gas 4. Grease and line the base of a loaf tin.

Drain and flake the salmon and mix in the lemon juice. Melt the butter in a pan, stir in the flour, add the milk and cream and bring to a boil stirring constantly. Simmer for 1 minute, then stir into the salmon mixture with the seasoning, egg, celery, herbs if using, and breadcrumbs. Spoon into the prepared tin and bake for 30 minutes. Cool slightly and turn out. Serve hot or cold, cut into slices. SERVES 6.

Variation

Replace the salmon with tuna fish for a change.

Scrummy Fish Pie

675 g / 1½ lb potatoes, peeled and halved
3 packets frozen cod in cheese sauce
75 g / 3 oz Cheddar cheese, grated
salt and pepper to taste

Cook the potatoes in salted water until tender. Drain thoroughly and mash until smooth.

Meanwhile, cook the fish according to the directions on the packet. When cooked, snip open the packets and drain the sauce into the mashed potatoes and stir to mix well. Flake the fish and stir in. Season to taste. Heat the grill. Spoon into an ovenproof baking dish and sprinkle with grated cheese. Grill until brown and bubbling. SERVES 4.

Variations

Replace one of the packets of cod in cheese sauce with 2 chopped hard-boiled eggs.

Another good idea is to replace the grated cheese topping with a small packet of lightly crushed crisps.

Kedgeree

225 g / 8 oz long grain brown or white rice
2 (280-g / 10-oz) packets boil-in-the-bag smoked haddock fillets
2 eggs
75 g / 3 oz butter or margarine
150 ml / ¼ pint single cream or creamy milk
salt and pepper to taste

Put the rice in a saucepan and add enough water to cover it by about 10 cm / 4 in. Add a pinch of salt, and bring to a boil. Simmer gently until the rice is tender – about 40 minutes for brown rice (15 minutes in a pressure cooker) and 15 minutes for white rice. Drain the cooked rice thoroughly, rinse with boiling water and drain again. Meanwhile, cook the smoked haddock according to the directions on the packet. Allow to cool slightly, then open the packet and tip the contents into a dish. Flake the fish using two forks. Keep any buttery juices from the fish but discard any skin and bones. Hard-boil the eggs, then cool them quickly by immersing them in cold water. Peel and coarsely chop.

Melt the butter or margarine in a heavy pan. Stir in the cooked rice and heat gently for 2 minutes, stirring occasionally. Stir in the flaked fish with its butter and juices, followed by the chopped eggs. Cook gently for 2 to 3 minutes, stirring frequently until the mixture is very hot. Stir in the cream, season to taste and serve immediately. SERVES 4.

Note: The quickest way to prepare this dish is to use cold, cooked rice left over from a previous meal, plus eggs and fish that have been cooked earlier. The smoked haddock can be replaced with kipper fillets.

Macaroni Special

225 g /8 oz wholewheat macaroni
1 (298-g /10½-oz) can condensed tomato soup
150 ml /¼ pint milk
225 g /8 oz grated Cheddar cheese
salt and pepper to taste
2 tomatoes, thinly sliced

Set the oven at hot, 220 C, 425 F, gas 7. Cook the macaroni in boiling salted water for 15 minutes, until tender. Drain and rinse with boiling water. Rinse out the saucepan and add the soup and the milk to the pan. Bring to a boil, stirring, then stir in the drained macaroni, two-thirds of the cheese and season to taste with salt and pepper. Turn into an ovenproof dish, sprinkle with the remaining cheese and decorate with the tomato slices. Bake in the heated oven for 10 to 15 minutes until bubbling and golden brown. SERVES 4.

Variation

For a delicious meal-in-a-moment (or not too many, anyway!) for 4, set 350 g /12 oz macaroni on to boil. While this is happening, crisp 100 g /4 oz streaky bacon in a frying pan, and beat 3 eggs in a bowl, seasoning lightly. Heat a serving dish in a moderate oven (180 C, 350 F, gas 4). When the macaroni is ready, tip it into the warmed dish with the bacon and egg, mix well and serve right away.

Salmon Saturday Special (page 39) with new potatoes and toasted flaked almonds, broccoli and Hasty Hollandaise (page 49).

Overleaf, at the back Special Fried Rice (page 78) and Bombay Potatoes (page 70); *centre*, Chinese Chicken (page 20) with spicy yogurt and cucumber wedges; *at the front*, Sweet and Sour Crispy Cod (page 38) and Curry Crumble (page 25).

VEGETABLES

Children usually have to be tempted or bribed to eat vegetables.
Here are a few ideas which may help.

Broad Beans. Peel, simmer 10 to 15 minutes. Drain and remove outer skin if wished. Serve the beans in a white sauce, adding a little dried ham or cooked bacon.

Runner Beans. String, slice and simmer for 5 minutes till still crisp. Drain. Add a little oil to a frying pan or wok and when hot stir-fry the beans, some drained and halved canned water chestnuts, and some beansprouts. Season with a few drops of soy sauce (illustrated on page 46).

Broccoli. Cook in boiling salted water for about 5 minutes, until just tender. Drain, serve with Hasty Hollandaise sauce (page 49).

Brussels Sprouts. Trim off outer leaves. Cook in boiling water for 10 to 15 minutes. Drain. Either fry, in butter, until brown and crispy, or stir into cheese sauce. Spoon into a baking dish. Sprinkle with grated cheese and brown under the grill.

Cabbage. Shred and simmer for about 5 minutes. Drain. Fry in a little oil, dripping or butter until brown and crispy. For a change, slice a few cold, cooked sausages and fry with the cabbage. To make Bubble and Squeak, add mashed potatoes and diced cold cooked lamb, beef or chicken to the pan with the cabbage. Fry until really crisp and brown.

Carrots. Peel and boil for 15 to 20 minutes until tender, adding a little sugar to the water. Drain and purée in a food mill or processor. Stir in a little butter, reheat if necessary and season to taste.

Cauliflower. Break into florets. Wash thoroughly and boil for 10 to 15 minutes until tender. Drain, reserving the water if wished to make a cheese sauce (mix half and half with milk) to make the good old standby, cauliflower cheese. To save time, put the cooked cauliflower in a heatproof baking dish and sprinkle with grated cheese and brown under the grill. Another idea is to fry cooked cauliflower until golden brown and crispy. If you have more time, dip cooked cauliflower in egg and coat with breadcrumbs and deep fry.

From the top A salad of runner beans with water chestnuts and bean sprouts (above), purée of spinach with buttered toast fingers (page 48), Purée of Carrots and Parsnips (page 50) and courgette fritters (page 48).

Chinese leaf. This makes one of the best salad ingredients: you get plenty for your money and it keeps extremely well in the bottom of the fridge. To please the children, slice it and some red pepper or onion, mix with pineapple chunks and mayonnaise (bought will do fine) and scatter with chopped nuts.

Courgettes. Slice and fry in butter with a few flaked almonds until golden brown and crisp, or dip in batter and deep fry.

Jerusalem artichokes. Peel, cook in boiling water for 5 minutes. Drain and roast with potatoes or around the joint.

Leeks. Trim and wash well. Slice and put into a well-buttered baking dish, with more butter dotted on top, salt and pepper. Cover and braise gently in a moderate oven (180 C, 350 F, gas 4) until tender – about 20 minutes.

Parsnips. Peel, quarter and boil for 2 minutes. Drain and roast with the potatoes or round the joint. (See also Purée of Carrots and Parsnips, page 50.)

Roast potatoes. To make the best roast potatoes, boil them first for 5 minutes in salted water, then peel them. Cut into halves or quarters if large or very large, score the surface with a fork to encourage a crisp finish, roll in flour and sprinkle with sea salt. About an hour before the end of the roasting time for your joint, pour some of the fat from around it into a separate pan, top it up with dripping or oil, put it into the oven to get good and hot, then add the potatoes and a few cloves of peeled garlic. Turn well in the fat to coat well, and do the same as often as you can remember during the cooking.

Spinach. Boil until tender. Drain thoroughly, then squeeze dry. Chop very finely or purée. Stir into cheese sauce. Serve with fingers of buttered toast.

Swedes. Peel and boil until tender. Mash and add to mashed potatoes. Add a little butter and season to taste.

Tomatoes. If you have a good supply of sweet, firm tomatoes, there is no simpler or better way of enjoying them than making an uncooked tomato sauce. To every $\frac{1}{2}$ kg / 1 lb of skinned, chopped tomatoes add a small chopped onion and, if you like, a mashed clove of garlic. Mix well, season and chill. Dress with a little oil and chopped parsley before serving with (very hot) spaghetti or tagliatelle. You could also mix with pasta shells or other shapes to make a cold pasta salad.

Hasty Hollandaise

Illustrated on page 43

1 tablespoon lemon juice or wine vinegar
2 teaspoons cold water
a little salt and pepper
3 egg yolks
175 g / 6 oz butter

Put the lemon juice, water, seasonings, and egg yolks in the blender. Heat the butter until almost boiling. Blend the yolk mixture briefly then slowly pour in the butter, blending all the time. If the mixture starts to curdle add an ice cube. SERVES 4.

Note: chopped fresh herbs added to the finished sauce give a wonderful flavour.

Purée of carrots and parsnips

Illustrated on page 46

450 g / 1 lb carrots, peeled and sliced
450 g / 1 lb parsnips, peeled and sliced
50 g / 2 oz butter or margarine
salt and pepper to taste

Put the vegetables in a pan of cold, salted water. Cover, bring to a boil and simmer until very tender – about 20 to 25 minutes.

Drain (but save the cooking water, it is excellent for making gravy or soup) the vegetables thoroughly. Purée in a food processor or blender or push through a sieve. Beat in the butter or margarine and a little salt and pepper to taste. Serve immediately. SERVES 4.

Peperonata

Serve this spicy, peppery stew hot with meat or fish, or cold as a salad.

4 tablespoons sunflower seed oil
1 large onion, chopped
4 large peppers (red, green or both), chopped
2 (397-g / 14-oz) cans chopped tomatoes
salt and black pepper

Heat the oil in a large, heavy pan. Add the onion and peppers, cover and cook gently until soft, about 15 minutes. Add the chopped tomatoes and their juice and season well with salt and pepper. Cook for another 30 minutes, uncovered this time, stirring occasionally. The tomato juices should have evaporated and the mixture become a rich stew. Check seasoning. SERVES 4 to 6.

Potato Gratin

1·5 kg / 3 lb potatoes, peeled
3 spring onions, sliced
175 g / 6 oz Cheddar cheese, grated
4 eggs, beaten
1 clove garlic, crushed
300 ml / $\frac{1}{2}$ pint soured cream
salt and pepper to taste
butter for greasing

Set the oven at 200 C, 400 F, gas 6. Grate the potatoes into a colander and squeeze thoroughly to remove any excess water. Mix with the spring onions, grated cheese, eggs, garlic and soured cream and add a little salt and pepper to taste.

Grease a shallow ovenproof baking dish and spoon the mixture into the dish. Bake in the heated oven for 35 minutes until crispy on top. SERVES 8.

PUDDINGS

Pudding is so often the high spot of a meal for all of us (but especially for dads, I find) that even the busiest mums will scarcely be forgiven for failing to produce one, particularly at weekends. However, this little selection should show you that a pudding need not be time-consuming to make, nor fattening to eat.

Brownie Pudding

150 g / 5 oz self-raising flour
175 g / 6 oz castor sugar
4 tablespoons cocoa powder
pinch of salt
6 tablespoons milk
a few drops vanilla essence
50 g / 2 oz melted butter
100 g / 4 oz chopped walnuts (optional)
175 g / 6 oz soft dark brown sugar
400 ml / 14 fl oz hot water

Set the oven at 180 C, 350 F, gas 4.

Grease a 20-cm / 7-in square baking dish or cake tin. Sift together the flour, castor sugar, 2 tablespoons cocoa powder and the salt. Stir in the milk, vanilla and melted butter and mix thoroughly. Stir in the nuts if using. Pour into the prepared tin. Mix together the brown sugar and remaining cocoa and sprinkle this mixture over the batter in the tin. Gently pour over the hot water. Bake for 40 to 45 minutes. SERVES 4.

Apple Meringue

Illustrated on page 55

4 large cooking apples
50 g / 2 oz castor sugar, or to taste
50 g / 2 oz raisins
1 egg, separated
2 egg whites
175 g / 6 oz castor sugar

Peel, core and thinly slice the apples. Put into a saucepan with a little water – enough to moisten and prevent the apples sticking. Cover and simmer gently, stirring frequently, until the apples are very soft – about 15 minutes. Set the oven at moderately hot, 200 C, 400 F, gas 6. Remove the pan from the heat and stir in the castor sugar to taste, the raisins and the egg yolk. Spoon into an ovenproof baking dish. Whisk the 3 egg whites until they stand in stiff peaks. Whisk in a third of the 175 g / 6 oz castor sugar, then gently fold in the remainder. Spoon on top of the apple purée and bake in the heated oven for 15 minutes. Serve hot or cold. Serves 4.

Variation

Special apple crumble. Replace the meringue topping with a crunchy crumble topping: sieve 100 g / 4 oz flour with a pinch of salt into a mixing bowl. Stir in 50 g / 2 oz ground almonds and 25 g / 1 oz demerara sugar. Rub in 100 g / 4 oz butter or hard margarine until the mixture resembles coarse breadcrumbs.

Mix the apple purée with 50 g / 2 oz chopped nuts and 1 teaspoon cinnamon. Replace the castor sugar in the purée with soft brown or demerara sugar. Replace the raisins with sultanas.

Sprinkle the crumble over the apple mixture and bake for 15 to 20 minutes until crisp and golden. Serves 4.

Note: Make a large quantity of apple purée and freeze in small portions to save time.

Chocolate Bread and Butter Pudding

500 ml / 17 fl oz creamy milk, or 150 ml / $\frac{1}{4}$ pint single cream plus
350 ml / 12 fl oz milk
3 large eggs
100 g / 4 oz castor sugar
100 g / 4 oz plain chocolate, chopped
3 slices bread
25 g / 1 oz butter, softened
25 g / 1 oz sultanas
castor sugar to dust

Set the oven at moderate, 180 C, 350 F, gas 4.

Grease a large pie dish. Put the milk in a pan and bring just to a boil. Whisk the eggs and sugar together in a large bowl then whisk in the hot milk. Add the chocolate and stir until dissolved. Butter the bread and cut the slices in half. Arrange in the pie dish, sprinkling the sultanas between and on top of the slices. Pour over the chocolate milk mixture. Stand the pie dish in a roasting tin half-filled with hot water then put the pudding in its water bath into the oven to bake for 40 to 45 minutes until set.

Remove the pie dish from the water bath and dust the top of the pudding with castor sugar. Serve hot or warm. SERVES 4 to 6.

Note: To make traditional Bread and Butter Pudding omit the chocolate and add a couple of drops of vanilla essence to the egg mixture.

Apple Meringue (page 53) and Fudge Banana Pie (page 60).

Banana Custard

600 ml / 1 pint milk
50 g / 2 oz castor sugar
few drops vanilla essence
3 eggs · 1 tablespoon cornflour
4 bananas

Put the milk, sugar and vanilla essence into a pan and bring slowly to the boil. Stir occasionally to dissolve the sugar. Whisk the eggs with the cornflour and, still whisking, pour the milk onto the egg mixture. Return the mixture to the pan and stir over low heat until the custard thickens. Do not allow to boil or the custard will curdle.

Remove from the heat and stir in the vanilla essence to taste. Allow to cool slightly. Meanwhile thickly slice the bananas. Carefully stir the bananas into the custard and pour the mixture into a serving dish. Allow to cool completely then serve with sponge fingers. SERVES 4.

But, if you are really up against it, and can't make a proper custard like this one, simply whisk up a packet of custard, and slice the bananas into it.

Yogurt Fool

Illustrated on page 33

300 ml / ½ pint plain yogurt
300 ml / ½ pint whipping cream, whipped
1 eating apple, sliced thinly
1 banana, sliced thinly
1 pear, sliced thinly
a few grapes, strawberries, or raspberries (optional)
50 g / 2 oz dark soft brown sugar

Stir the yogurt into the whipped cream then fold in the prepared fruits. Spoon into a serving dish and sprinkle with the sugar. Chill in the fridge for about 2 hours. SERVES 4.

Tatin Pudding (page 58) and cherry Jalousie (page 59).

Tatin Pudding

Illustrated on page 56

Packet sponge cake mix can be used to make a quick and easy hot pudding. Basically, just eggs, butter and water are added to the packet mix, saving time in weighing out ingredients and mixing. With a bit of imagination a packet mix can be a super pud!
Sologne in the Loire region of France is famous for its Tarte Tatin, an upside-down caramelised apple pie. I've discovered that a sponge topping is just as delicious.

50 g / 2 oz butter
100 g / 4 oz castor sugar
450 g / 1 lb Golden Delicious apples
vanilla sponge cake mix, which usually requires:
2 eggs and 50 g / 2 oz butter
2 teaspoons water to make up sponge

Set the oven at moderately hot, 190 C, 375 F, gas 5.

Lightly grease an 18-cm / 7-in deep cake tin or ovenproof dish. Put the butter and sugar in a heavy pan and cook slowly, stirring occasionally, until the mixture turns a golden caramel colour. Pour into the cake tin.

Meanwhile, peel, core and quarter the apples. Arrange the apples on top of the hot caramel. Place in the oven and make up the sponge cake mix according to the directions on the packet, using the eggs and water and butter. Remove the cake tin from the oven and pour the pudding mixture over the apples. Return the tin to the oven and bake for a further 30 to 35 minutes until the pudding is golden and firm to the touch. Run a knife around the edge of the pudding, place a large serving plate over the tin and invert the tin so that pudding and apple topping fall onto the plate. Spoon any apple or caramel that may have stuck to the tin onto the pudding. Serve hot or warm with cream or ice cream. SERVES 4 to 6.

Jalousie

Illustrated on page 56

2 (85-g / 3 oz) sheets frozen puff pastry (half of a
340-g / 12-oz packet)
FILLING
675 g / 1½ lb cooking apples, peeled, cored and sliced
50 g / 2 oz castor sugar, or to taste
grated rind of 1 lemon
1 egg, beaten to glaze

Leave the pastry to thaw at room temperature for 10 minutes. Meanwhile, prepare the filling. Mix the sliced apples with the sugar and lemon rind. Set the oven at 220 C, 425 F, gas 7.

Roll out each sheet to a rectangle 30 × 25 cm / 12 × 10 in and 1·5 mm / $\frac{1}{16}$ in thick. Place one rectangle on a baking sheet and cover with an even layer of the apple filling, leaving a border 1 cm / ½ in wide on all sides. Brush the border with a little beaten egg. Fold the remaining rectangle of pastry in half lengthways to make a strip 30 × 13 cm / 12 × 5 in. Using a sharp knife, cut across the fold to within 1 cm / ½ in of the edge. Continue cutting slits at 1-cm / ½-in intervals. Open the folded pastry out and, using a rolling pin, lift the pastry on top of the first sheet covered with apple. Press the edges to seal. Lightly brush the top with beaten egg and bake in the heated oven for 25 minutes, reducing the temperature to 190 C, 375 F, gas 5 after 15 minutes.

Serve warm or cold, sprinkled with a little sugar. SERVES 4 to 6.

Variations

1. **Cherry filling.** Replace the apple filling with 225 g / 8 oz frozen or stoned and drained canned cherries.
2. **Dutch apple filling.** Replace the castor sugar with dark or light soft brown sugar, omit the lemon rind and add 1 teaspoon ground cinnamon and 50 g / 2 oz raisins or sultanas or a few chopped nuts.
3. **Mincemeat and apple filling.** Peel, core and chop 225 g / ½ lb cooking apples and mix with a 225 g / 8 oz jar mincemeat.

Another quick, and very good, variation is simply to spread the pastry base with jam, marmalade or lemon curd.

Fudge Banana Pie

Illustrated on page 55

1 (397-g / 14-oz) can condensed milk
75 g / 3 oz butter or margarine, melted
175 g / 6 oz digestive biscuits, crushed
50 g / 2 oz walnuts, chopped
2 bananas

Put the unopened can of condensed milk in a pan of cold water. Bring to a boil, then cover and simmer gently for 3 hours; be careful to check the water level from time to time, and top up if necessary. Remove the can from the water and allow to cool completely.

Mix together the melted butter, digestive biscuits and walnuts and press onto the base and up the sides of a 23-cm / 9-in flan dish or spring-clip tin. Open the can of milk – it will have turned into a sticky brown fudge sauce. Pour into the flan case. Peel and slice the bananas and arrange on top of the fudge filling. Serve immediately with ice cream. SERVES 4 to 6.

Note. This requires a little forward planning, but is very quickly assembled, and tastes really heavenly. The filling can also be used as a sauce for ice cream or sponge puddings.

Redlands Farm Rice Pudding

There is very little to beat a good rice pudding. A friend from Somerset is famous for this recipe.

40 g / 1½ oz butter
50 g / 2 oz round grain pudding rice
600 ml / 1 pint gold-top milk
25 g / 1 oz sugar, or to taste
1 vanilla pod or a little grated orange rind

Set the oven at 160 C, 325 F, gas 3. Use 15 g / ½ oz of the butter to grease thickly an ovenproof glass dish. Put the rice, milk and sugar and vanilla or orange rind into the dish, and stir gently to mix. Cut up the remaining butter and use to 'dot' the pudding.

Place in the heated oven for 2 hours, stirring the pudding after one hour. In this way, the pudding forms a lovely brown skin.

Serve with fruit and a little extra cream or evaporated milk. SERVES 4.

Mango Brulée

1 mango, peeled, stoned and cut into strips
50 g / 2 oz soft light brown sugar
300 g / 10 oz hazelnut yogurt
2 tablespoons dark brown sugar

Put the mango in a pan with the sugar and heat for 3 minutes. Spoon into 4 ramekins and cover with the yogurt. Sprinkle with the dark brown sugar and place under a hot grill for 3 minutes. Serve immediately. SERVES 4.

Figgy Pudding

175 g / 6 oz brown bread, cut into small cubes
175 ml / 6 fl oz milk
1 medium cooking apple, peeled, cored and sliced
25 g / 1 oz soft brown sugar
$\frac{1}{2}$ teaspoon cinnamon
2 tablespoons thick cut marmalade
75 g / 3 oz dried figs, chopped
1 tablespoon raisins
1 tablespoon chopped nuts (almonds, walnuts or hazelnuts)
50 g / 2 oz butter, melted
1 egg, beaten

Set the oven at 180 C, 350 F, gas 4. Grease an ovenproof baking dish.

Soak the bread in the milk until soft, then mash it with a fork. Arrange the apple slices in the base of the dish and sprinkle with half the brown sugar and the cinnamon. Stir the remaining ingredients into the bread mixture and spoon on top of the apples. Bake in the heated oven for 1 hour. Sprinkle with a little castor sugar, if liked, and serve warm or cold with custard or ice cream. SERVES 4.

Suppers

There have been times in our history when those of us fortunate enough to be able to do so used to eat huge amounts of food at every meal. Breakfast sideboards were laden with silver salvers of kedgeree, poached eggs, devilled kidneys and the like. Luncheon had at least three courses, and was followed by tea at four o'clock, which probably consisted of bread and butter, sandwiches, small cakes and a large fruit cake. Then at eight the family would sit down to a gigantic four-course dinner. However did they manage to devour it all and survive? I doubt if I could manage two large meals a day now; what with dieting and often just having time for a snack at lunchtime, my stomach seems to have shrunk.

If the family have sat down to a large main meal in the middle of the day, as on Sundays, it is often better to have a small and simple meal in the evenings. Supper is usually a cosy, relaxing repast, and should be a pleasant preliminary to bedtime, with the younger children bathed and in their dressing gowns ready to be whisked upstairs the moment it's over. Here are some supper recipes which are easy to prepare and, hopefully, won't cause indigestion or bad dreams.

Beans Means Pasties

Illustrated on page 73

*Whenever heating baked beans I add a good dollop of tomato ketchup.
It gives the sauce a really good flavour and a much better colour.*

1 (340-g / 12-oz) packet 4 puff pastry sheets
1 (450-g / 15¾-oz) can baked beans with mini frankfurters
1 egg, beaten

Set the oven at 220 C, 425 F, gas 7. Thaw the pastry sheets at room
temperature for 10 minutes. Drain the beans and frankfurters. The
liquid can be served separately as a sauce.

Roll out each pastry square to an oblong. Cut each oblong in half
to give two squares. Place a spoonful of filling in the centre of each
square. Brush the edges with beaten egg and fold the squares in
half to form a triangle. Press the edges with a fork to seal firmly.
Transfer to a baking sheet and brush the triangles with beaten egg.
Bake in the heated oven for 15 minutes until golden brown. Makes
8 pasties. SERVES 4 to 6.

Variations

1. Use a 450-g / 15¾-oz can of plain baked beans, but add to them
100 g / 4 oz sautéed and chopped chicken livers.
2. For a different, lighter filling, drain 2 (212-g / 7½-oz) tins of
button mushrooms, mix with a few tablespoons of double cream
and season well with salt and black pepper. Fill the puff pastry
squares and complete as above.

Neapolitan Pizza

Shops now sell ready-made pizza bases which can be quickly topped and baked. The basic topping recipe can be used for bought pizza bases, on pitta bread, halved baps or slices of French bread. This recipe makes enough topping for 4 pitta breads or 2 20-cm /8-in bases.

TOPPING
1 (310-g /10·9-oz) can Italian-style (Napoletana) tomato sauce
1 clove garlic, crushed (optional)
1 teaspoon dried oregano
2 to 3 spring onions, finely sliced
100 g /4 oz Mozzarella cheese, sliced
1 (49-g /1¾-oz) can anchovy fillets, drained
3 to 4 black olives

Set the oven at 220 C, 425 F, gas 7. Mix the sauce with the garlic, oregano and onions. Spread on the pizza base, pitta breads, or French bread. Lay the cheese slices on top and decorate with anchovy fillets and olives. Bake in the heated oven for 5 minutes until bubbling.

Variations

1. Replace the anchovies with a few slices of salami or peperoni, and use a few capers instead of olives.
2. Add ½ green pepper, diced, to the sauce mixture with the onions.
3. Replace the anchovies with a few ounces of diced ham or bacon or garlic sausage, or a few drained, canned sardines.

Lamb Burgers

1 (300-g / 10-oz) packet frozen chopped spinach, thawed
450 g / 1 lb lean minced lamb, uncooked
50 g / 2 oz fresh brown breadcrumbs
2 eggs, beaten
pinch each cumin and ground coriander
salt and pepper
2 spring onions, chopped
oil for frying

Squeeze all the excess liquid from the spinach and mix with all the remaining ingredients except the oil, adding a little salt and pepper. Stir until thoroughly mixed. Shape into 4 burgers. Heat the oil in a large frying pan and fry the burgers for 4 to 5 minutes on each side. Drain thoroughly and serve with a spicy tomato sauce. SERVES 4.

Tuna Will-Will

*Will-Will is a 41-year-old American child who grew up in Kensington.
He says this recipe is made all over the United States, and I think it
deserves to be better known here. Apart from being extremely quick and
easy to put together, it is also very tasty.*

1 (298-g / 10½-oz) can Campbell's cream of mushroom soup,
undiluted
1 (198-g / 7-oz) can tuna, flaked
1 (75-g / 2·6-oz) packet potato crisps

Set the oven at moderately hot, 190 C, 375 F, gas 5. Mix together
the condensed soup, tuna and the crisps, lightly crushed. Put all
this into an ovenproof dish and cook in the heated oven –
uncovered if you want the top to be nice and crisp – for 25 minutes
or so.

Noodles with Ham and Cheese

350 g / 12 oz quick-cook egg noodles
50 g / 2 oz butter
100 g / 4 oz ham, diced
175 g / 6 oz cheese (Cheddar, Gruyère, Brie, Camembert) grated
or diced
salt and pepper to taste

Cook the noodles in boiling salted water according to the
instructions on the packet. Drain thoroughly, rinse with hot water
and drain again. Return to the pan with the butter and heat gently,
stirring now and then, until melted. Stir in the ham, cheese and salt
and pepper to taste. Toss gently over low heat until thoroughly
mixed and hot through. Serve immediately. SERVES 4.

Bentley Family Fish Bake

This is a simple recipe to make with tinned salmon, and because it takes no chewing it is excellent for little children, old people or invalids. Serve with a green vegetable.

1 kg / 2 lb old potatoes
75 ml / 2½ fl oz milk
100 g / 4 oz butter
1 (213-g / 7½-oz) can salmon
1 egg, beaten
anchovy essence
salt and pepper
tomato ketchup
1 tomato, sliced
50 g / 2 oz grated cheese

Set the oven at 180 C, 350 F, gas 4.

Peel, then boil the potatoes in salted water, and mash them with the milk and 75 g / 3 oz of the butter. Add the salmon and egg and beat the mixture well until it's nice and creamy. Add a few drops of anchovy essence, salt and pepper and quite a lot of tomato ketchup. Test and taste until the flavour is good (it should look pale pink). Spoon it into a greased oven dish, make patterns on the top with a fork and dot with the rest of the butter. Arrange the tomato slices on top and sprinkle with the grated cheese. Bake in the heated oven for 30 to 40 minutes. If you prefer it, or for a change, use tuna fish.
SERVES 4 to 6.

Crispy Potato Omelette

Illustrated on page 74

This is a marvellous way to use up left-over boiled, baked or roast potatoes. For a change, stir in a few cooked peas, diced cooked carrots, sliced tomatoes (or virtually any vegetable), diced or grated cheese, diced ham or cooked meat.

4 large eggs, beaten
2 tablespoons milk or water
salt and pepper to taste
25 g / 1 oz butter
about 2 medium, cooked potatoes cut in chunks

Beat the eggs with the milk or water and a little salt and pepper until frothy. Heat the butter in a frying pan and fry the potatoes until brown and crispy. Stir in the egg mixture, and cook, stirring gently until set. Fold in half. Slide onto a plate and serve quickly. SERVES 2.

Variation

Another idea is to add a few chopped rashers of streaky bacon to the pan with the potatoes.

Bombay Potatoes

Illustrated on pages 44-5

*This is the perfect way to start children on curried dishes, because even
though it is deliciously spicy, it is not too much so; neither is it hot.
It was a special childhood favourite of an Indian friend from Bombay,
and the recipe comes from their cook, who is still with his family today.*

675 g / 1½ lb new potatoes
oil for frying
1 large clove of garlic
2 teaspoons mustard seeds
½ teaspoon turmeric
1 teaspoon chilli powder
1 teaspoon salt
4 eggs
chopped fresh coriander or parsley for garnish

Peel and cube the potatoes quite small (about the size of a
Monopoly dice). Heat the oil in a large frying pan and add the
garlic and mustard seeds. When the garlic sizzles and the mustard
seeds start to pop, add the potatoes and turn them over until they
are coated in the oil and spicy mixture. Add the turmeric, chilli
powder and salt, stir well, then cover and cook, stirring
occasionally, for 15 to 20 minutes.

Next, make 4 holes in the potatoes with the back of a spoon,
break an egg into each, return to the heat, cover and cook for 5 to
10 minutes more. Sprinkle with chopped fresh coriander or parsley
before serving. SERVES 4.

Note. Without the final addition of the eggs, Bombay Potatoes
make an ideal accompaniment to mild meat curries.

David's Savoury Avocados

Illustrated on page 73

4 ripe avocados
25 g / 1 oz butter
3 (120-g / 4½-oz) cans sardines in tomato sauce
or 2 (184-g / 6½-oz) cans tuna, drained
1 teaspoon dried mixed herbs
100 g / 4 oz mushrooms, halved
2 teaspoons tomato purée
3 tablespoons water or white wine
pepper to taste
dash each of Tabasco and Worcestershire sauce

Set the oven at 190 C, 375 F, gas 5. Cut the avocados in half, remove their stones and peel them. Lay the avocado halves in a shallow baking dish in a single layer and bake in the heated oven for 5 minutes while preparing the filling. Melt the butter in a frying pan, add the remaining ingredients and cook, stirring until thick and tasty – about 4 minutes.

Spoon into the warm avocados and serve immediately with a green salad. SERVES 4.

Note. For smaller children, who may find the sardine filling a little too rich at supper time, tuna makes the ideal alternative.

Chicken and Sweet Corn Loaf

25 g / 1 oz butter
1 medium onion, chopped
225 g / 8 oz boneless uncooked chicken or turkey
100 g / 4 oz streaky bacon
100 g / 4 oz pork sausagemeat
1 (312-g / 11-oz) can creamstyle corn
1 egg, beaten
75 g / 3 oz fresh breadcrumbs
salt and pepper to taste

Set the oven at 180 C, 350 F, gas 4. Grease and line the base of a 0·5-kg / 1-lb loaf tin. Melt the butter in a frying pan. Add the onion and cook slowly, stirring occasionally, for 5 minutes. Meanwhile, cut the chicken or turkey meat into small cubes. Remove the rind from the bacon and chop it. Add the chicken and bacon to the frying pan and stir-fry over medium heat for 5 minutes.

Remove from the heat and stir in the remaining ingredients. Spoon into the prepared tin and bake in the heated oven for 1 hour. SERVES 4 to 6.

This loaf is very good either hot or cold, with baked jacket potatoes.

David's Savoury Avocado (page 71) with a Chinese leaf salad (page 48) and Beans Means Pasties (page 64).

Isabella's Sausage Supper

Matteson's smoked sausage rings are tasty and nourishing. It's a good idea to keep a couple handy. They have a long fridge life and can be used in casseroles and stews. I once had an au pair girl, Isabella, who concocted this supper (or lunch) dish and it was relished by all the family, so I've named it after her.

2 sausage rings
1 small onion, finely chopped
2 tablespoons French mustard
2 tablespoons tomato ketchup
1 kg /2 lb potatoes, boiled and creamily mashed with
butter and milk
1 or 2 (142-g /5-oz) packets frozen small onions in white sauce
1 tomato, sliced
50 g /2 oz grated cheese

Set the oven at 180C, 350F, gas 4. Cut the sausages into pieces about 7·5 cm /3 inches in length. Then cut them lengthwise, but not right through. Mix the onion with the French mustard and tomato ketchup. Fill the cuts with this mixture and arrange the sausage pieces on the bottom of a greased oven dish. Cover it all with mashed potato. Make a well in the middle. Make up the frozen onions, using slightly less water than stated (use two packets if it's for a family, or a large dish). Pour the onions with their sauce into the well. Cover them with slices of tomato. Using a fork, make the mashed potato look pretty round the edges of the dish and sprinkle with the grated cheese. Bake in the heated oven for 30 to 40 minutes. SERVES 6.

Lone Ranger Beef and Pronto (page 76) and Crispy Potato Omelette (page 69).

Lone Ranger Beef and Pronto

Illustrated on page 74

This excellent little supper dish takes about 12 minutes to prepare.

225 g / 8 oz rice
2 tablespoons oil
450 g / 1 lb very lean minced beef
1 onion, finely sliced
100 g / 4 oz mushrooms, quartered
1 (298-g / 10½-oz) can condensed tomato soup
2 tablespoons tomato purée
salt and pepper to taste
150 ml / ¼ pint plain yogurt

Cook the rice in boiling salted water till soft, then drain and rinse with boiling water. Drain again thoroughly. Meanwhile, heat the oil in a large frying pan. Add the meat and quickly stir-fry over high heat until browned. Stir in the onion and mushrooms. Reduce the heat and cook for 5 minutes, stirring frequently. Add the soup, tomato purée and a little salt and pepper to taste. Stir well to mix, bring to the boil and simmer gently for 3 to 4 minutes. Stir in the yogurt and serve on a bed of rice. SERVES 4.

Bacon and Parsnip Bake

25 g / 1 oz butter
4 bacon chops
1 large onion, sliced
675 g / 1½ lb parsnips, peeled and sliced
a little pepper to taste
300 ml / ½ pint chicken stock
50 g / 2 oz cheese, grated

Set the oven at 180 C, 350 F, gas 4. Melt the butter in a frying pan and fry the chops on both sides until browned. Remove from the pan and add the onion. Cook gently for 5 minutes then add the parsnips and cook for 2 minutes; stirring frequently. Sprinkle with a little pepper.

Spoon half the vegetable mixture into an ovenproof casserole, lay the chops on top and cover with the remaining vegetables. Pour over the stock and sprinkle with the cheese. Bake in the heated oven for 45 minutes or until the parsnips are browned and tender. SERVES 4.

Delicious Drumsticks

8 chicken drumsticks
4 tablespoons tomato ketchup
1 teaspoon wine vinegar
1 teaspoon mustard
1 teaspoon dark brown sugar
4 tablespoons olive oil
3 teaspoons Worcestershire sauce

Heat the grill. Using a sharp knife, make several deep slashes in the skin of the drumsticks. Mix all the remaining ingredients together and coat the drumsticks. Grill the chicken until crispy and the meat is tender (about 10 to 15 minutes depending on the heat of your grill), turning frequently. Serve hot, with Sticky Rice (page 107) or cold with a rice salad (page 132). SERVES 4.

Special Fried Rice

Illustrated on pages 44-5

5 tablespoons vegetable oil
1 egg, beaten
2 tablespoons chopped spring onions
1 clove garlic, chopped
1 teaspoon chopped root ginger
100 g / 4 oz frozen prawns, thawed
$\frac{1}{2}$ teaspoon cornflour
salt
dash of sherry
100 g / 4 oz back bacon, cut into strips
50 g / 2 oz frozen peas, thawed
275 g / 10 oz American long grain rice, cooked
1 tablespoon soy sauce

Heat 2 tablespoons of the oil in a wok or large frying pan. Mix the egg with half the spring onions and a pinch of salt. Pour into the wok or frying pan and quickly fry to make an omelette. Turn out onto a plate and cut into thin strips. Add another tablespoon of oil to the wok and fry the garlic and ginger very gently for 30 seconds, add the prawns mixed with the cornflour and a pinch of salt, add a dash of sherry and stir-fry for 1 minute. Tip out onto a plate. Add another $\frac{1}{2}$ teaspoon of oil to the wok, add the bacon and stir-fry for 2 minutes, add the peas and stir-fry for another 2 minutes. Tip out on to the plate. Wipe out the wok or pan and add the remaining oil. When heated, add the rice and stir-fry for 3 minutes. Add the soy sauce, stir well, then stir in remaining ingredients. Fry for 1 minute. Garnish with the remaining chopped spring onion. SERVES 4.

Snacks

When I was small and asked in between meals for a 'snack', my mother used to say: 'All right, I'll get the dog to bite you.' 'Snack' is a marvellously descriptive word for a small meal, and although I frown on eating in between meals because it kills the appetite, it is sometimes necessary to put something into a child's stomach if the main meal is being delayed or if there isn't time for a child to have a full meal before dashing off to some social or educational function. It's much better to give the child something wholesome rather than a packet of crisps or, even worse, sweets. Not that I'm totally against cakes or sweets — it would be a dull life if we were not allowed *some* treats or delights to look forward to — but sugary things play the devil with teeth, and rationing them is one way of preventing caries. Cleaning teeth after eating sweet things should be encouraged, but if this is not possible give a piece of cheese to nibble, it is an excellent way of neutralising the harmful effects of sugar. If a child is whining about being hungry, it's a good idea to offer a little fruit, a stick of celery, or a raw carrot, rather than the biscuit tin.

Here are a few suggestions for quick, easy tummy fillers to ward off hunger pangs. Some of them can be served as high tea, Saturday lunch, or as a light supper.

Mackerel Pâté

Illustrated on page 91

225 g / 8 oz cooked smoked mackerel fillets
lemon juice to taste
pepper to taste
85 g / 3½ oz 'Philly' cheese

Skin and flake the fish. Mash thoroughly until smooth with the lemon juice, pepper and cream cheese. Spoon into individual ramekins or into a small bowl. Chill until ready to serve with hot toast or crackers.

Variation

Replace the mackerel with a 225-g / 8-oz can salmon or tuna fish, drained and flaked.

Cheesy Bunnies

Illustrated on page 91

4 hamburger buns or baps
50 g / 2 oz soft butter or margaine
50 g / 2 oz diced ham or cooked bacon (optional)
4 eggs
4 slices processed cheese

Set the oven at 160 C, 325 F, gas 3. Then, using a 3·5-5 cm / 1½-2 in biscuit cutter, cut a circle out of the centre of each bun, cutting to within 1 cm / ½ in of the bottom of the bun. Butter the hole inside the bun, spoon the ham into the holes. Place the buns on a baking sheet and crack an egg into the hole in each bun. Bake in the heated oven for 25 minutes. Remove and cover the top of each bun and egg with a slice of cheese. Return to the oven and cook for a further 5 minutes. SERVES 4.

Croque Monsieur

4 slices bread · 4 slices processed cheese
2 slices ham · 15 g / $\frac{1}{2}$ oz butter · oil for frying

Make 2 sandwiches in the following way: bread, slice cheese, slice ham, slice cheese and bread again. Press down firmly. Melt the butter with a little oil in a heavy frying pan. Add the 2 sandwiches and fry over medium heat for 2 minutes on each side until golden and crispy. Drain well on kitchen paper and serve quickly. SERVES 2.

Croque Madame

Fry the sandwiches as above, and top each one with a fried or poached egg.

Welsh Rarebit

100 g / 4 oz well-flavoured hard cheese, grated
$\frac{1}{2}$ teaspoon made mustard
15 g / $\frac{1}{2}$ oz butter · 2 slices bread, toasted

Mix the cheese with the mustard and butter and spread onto the toast. Grill until golden brown and bubbling. SERVES 2.

London Rarebit

100 g / 4 oz 'Philly' cheese · 1 tablespoon chutney
1 stalk celery, chopped · 2 slices bread, toasted

Mix the cheese with the chutney and celery. If wished add a few drops of Worcestershire sauce. Spread onto the toast and grill until light brown. SERVES 2.

EGG DISHES

Here are a few quick egg snacks that should happily fill a few holes.

Eggs en Cocotte

25 g / 1 oz butter
4 large eggs
salt and pepper
4 tablespoons cream

Set the oven at 180 C, 350 F, gas 4. Use the butter to grease four ramekin dishes. Break an egg into each, season with a little salt and pepper, and top with a tablespoon of cream. Put the dishes into a roasting tin half-filled with hot water. Bring to the boil on top of the stove then bake in the heated oven for 10 minutes. If liked, brown under a hot grill. Serve immediately with sliced ham. SERVES 4.

Variations

1. Dice 175 g / 6 oz cheese and divide between the ramekins, break an egg on top and finish as the recipe above.

2. Slice 4 cold, cooked sausages or frankfurters and arrange them in the base of the ramekins before adding the eggs.

3. Flake 175 g / 6 oz cooked smoked haddock, kippers or mackerel, and place in the ramekins before adding the eggs.

All Kinds of Scrambled Eggs

8 large eggs
150 ml / $\frac{1}{4}$ pint soured cream or top of the milk
salt and pepper to taste
50 g / 2 oz butter

Whisk the eggs with the cream and seasonings. Heat the butter in a large, heavy pan and add the eggs, stirring briskly until the mixture thickens. The best scrambled eggs are cooked very slowly. Serve with hot, buttered toast and crispy bacon. SERVES 4.

Variations

1. Add a little mustard powder and a few drops of Worcestershire sauce and a pinch of cayenne pepper to the eggs with the cream.

2. Add 50 g / 2 oz diced or grated cheese to the mixture just before it is ready to serve.

3. Add a little diced ham or smoked salmon to the mixture before serving.

4. Add 2 diced, skinned tomatoes and 1 tablespoon chopped chives before serving.

5. Add a little diced tofu (beancurd) to the eggs with the cream.

6. Stir in a few fried mushrooms before serving.

7. Add a tin of asparagus tips, drained, just before serving.

8. Soften a small onion and a red pepper, chopped, in the butter before adding the eggs.

9. Add a little chopped, cooked spinach to the eggs before serving.

Pain Chocolat and Frankfurter Rolls

Using a packet of white bread mix you can make 8 pain chocolat and 8 frankfurter rolls very quickly – they can be frozen unbaked or after they have been baked and cooled.
Pain Chocolat is the traditional snack given to children in France as they come out of school. This quick version uses bread dough instead of the usual croissant mixture.

1 (567-g / 1-lb 4-oz) packet white bread mix

Pain Chocolat

oil for greasing baking sheets
4 Mars Bars
2 tablespoons milk to glaze

Frankfurter Rolls

oil for greasing baking sheets
8 small frankfurters
2 tablespoons milk to glaze

Set the oven at hot, 230 C, 450 F, gas 8 and grease several baking sheets. Make up the bread dough according to the instructions on the packet. Knead well on a floured table for 5 minutes until smooth and elastic. Divide the dough into 16 equal pieces.

To make the Pain Chocolat, cut each Mars Bar in half lengthwise to make 8 'fingers' and place in the freezer until hard. Take 8 of the pieces of dough and pat each into a 10-cm / 4-in square. Roll each square of dough around a finger of Mars Bar, like a Swiss roll. Place the rolls, seam side down and placed well apart, on the baking sheets. Cover with a damp cloth and leave to rise in a warm place for about 20 minutes or until doubled in size. Brush with milk and bake in the heated oven for 10 to 15 minutes until golden.

To make the Frankfurter Rolls, pat each of the remaining portions of dough into a rectangle 15 × 7·5 cm / 6 × 3 in. Roll up each frankfurter in a rectangle of dough, like a giant sausage roll. Place the rolls, seam side underneath, on greased baking sheets, cover and leave to rise as above and bake in the heated oven for 10 to 12 minutes until golden.

Toasted Treats
(and pancake fillings too)

To make 2 toasted sandwiches, take 4 slices bread, buttered (buttered side out, touching the grill) and fill with the Welsh Rarebit mixture (page 81) mixed with:

198 g/7 oz can tuna, drained and flaked

or

100 g/4 oz frozen prawns, thawed

or

1 (198-g/7-oz) can sweet corn with peppers, drained

or

2 slices ham, diced

or

4 rashers bacon, grilled and chopped

or

100 g/4 oz diced cooked chicken and 2 chopped spring onions, or 1 tablespoon chutney

or

2 hard boiled eggs, chopped, and 2 tomatoes peeled, seeded and diced

or

4 slices salami, cut in strips, and a little diced red or green pepper

or

100 g/4 oz cooked smoked fish (haddock, cod or kippers), flaked

SERVES 2.

Pancakes

For 4 stuffed pancakes, fill as above, and bake in a buttered dish in a moderately hot oven (190 C, 375 F, gas 5) for 10 to 12 minutes.

Sticky Fingers

BASE
250 g /9 oz plain flour
75 g /3 oz icing sugar
pinch of salt
175 g /6 oz butter or margarine
TOPPING
4 large eggs, beaten
350 g /12 oz castor sugar
4 tablespoons lemon juice
1½ teaspoons grated lemon rind
50 g /2 oz flour
1 teaspoon baking powder

Set the oven at 180 C, 350 F, gas 4, and grease a deep Swiss roll or cake tin 23 × 32 × 5 cm /9 × 13 × 2 in.

First prepare the base. Sift the flour, icing sugar and salt into a bowl, then rub in the butter until the mixture resembles coarse crumbs. Using the back of a spoon, press the mixture into the prepared tin. Bake in the heated oven for 15 to 20 minutes until golden. Cool in the tin for 10 to 15 minutes while preparing the topping. Beat the eggs until frothy then gradually beat in the sugar, then lemon juice and rind. Sift over the flour and baking powder and stir into the mixture. Pour over the base. Bake for 25 to 30 minutes until firm. Cool in the tin before cutting into fingers. Store in an airtight tin.

Waffles

225 g / 8 oz plain flour
4 teaspoons baking powder
$\frac{1}{2}$ teaspoon salt
$1\frac{1}{2}$ teaspoons sugar
2 eggs
450 ml / $\frac{3}{4}$ pint milk
100 g / 4 oz butter or margarine, melted

Sift the dry ingredients together into a bowl.

Beat together the eggs, milk and melted butter and stir into the dry mixture. Beat to make a smooth, fairly thin batter. Cook in a hot waffle maker. MAKES 10 WAFFLES.

Variations

1. Choc-chip waffles. Stir 50 g / 2 oz chocolate chips into the batter before cooking.

2. Chocolate waffles. Sift 25 g / 1 oz cocoa powder and 50 g / 2 oz castor sugar with the dry ingredients. Serve with ice cream and hot chocolate sauce.

3. Cornflake waffles. Substitute 25 g / 1 oz crushed cornflakes for 25 g / 1 oz of the flour. Stir into the mixture before cooking.

4. Fairy Waffles. Add 2 tablespoons orange juice and 1 tablespoon grated orange rind to the mixture.

Pain Perdu

Illustrated on page 91

This is a good way to use up stale bread and does wonders for poorly children.

4 thick slices of bread
2 tablespoons castor sugar
150 ml / $\frac{1}{4}$ pint milk
1 egg, beaten
50 g / 2 oz butter
4 tablespoons jam
2 tablespoons water
icing sugar for dusting

Cut the crusts off the bread, then cut each slice in half. Dissolve the sugar in the milk. Put the bread into a shallow dish and pour the milk mixture over. Leave to soak for 5 minutes. Gently squeeze the milk out of the bread, then dip the bread in the beaten egg, making sure all the sides are well coated. Heat the butter in a frying pan and fry the bread for 1 to $1\frac{1}{2}$ minutes on each side, until crisp and golden.

Meanwhile, heat the jam with the water, stirring to make a smooth sauce. Drain the fried bread on absorbent paper and arrange on dessert plates. Dust with icing sugar and serve immediately with the jam sauce. SERVES 4.

French Cinnamon Toast

French cinnamon toast is a delicious treat, a variation on Pain Perdu that is very easy to make as a snack or dessert. You will need 1 or 2 thick slices of bread per person. For 8 slices, then, beat together 2 eggs and 300 ml / $\frac{1}{2}$ pint milk. Dip the bread into the mixture until it's good and soggy. Melt a knob of butter in a frying pan, and when it's quite hot fry the eggy bread until golden on both sides. Put onto warm plates and sprinkle with castor sugar and powdered cinnamon. It is also mouth-watering with golden syrup, maple syrup or jam.

Bugs Bunny's Carrot Cake

A really popular cake in the U.S., this is also a very healthy one.

1 teaspoon ground mixed spice
250 g / 9 oz wholemeal flour
large pinch of salt
2 teaspoons baking powder
150 g / 5 oz soft light brown sugar
2 ripe bananas, mashed
175 g / 6 oz carrots, grated
50 g / 2 oz raisins
3 large eggs, beaten
200 ml / 7 fl oz sunflower seed oil

Set the oven at 180 C, 350 F, gas 4, and grease and line the base of a cake tin 20 × 30 × 3·5 cm / 8 × 12 × 1½ in. Mix the spice, flour, salt and baking powder together in a mixing bowl. Make a well in the centre and add the sugar, mashed bananas, grated carrots, raisins, eggs and oil. Beat well until thoroughly mixed. Spoon into the prepared tin and bake in the heated oven for 30 to 40 minutes. Turn onto a wire rack to cool. Cut into squares.

Rib-sticking Parkin

Illustrated opposite

175 g /6 oz butter or margarine
175 g /6 oz wholemeal flour
225 g /8 oz soft brown sugar
2 teaspoons baking powder
65 g /2½ oz porridge oats
175 g /6 oz mixed dried fruit
50 g /2 oz chopped mixed nuts · 1 egg, beaten

Set the oven at 180 C, 350 F, gas 4, and grease a cake tin 20 × 30 × 3·5 cm /8 × 12 × 1½ in with a little of the butter, melt the rest of it. Put all the remaining ingredients in a bowl and mix thoroughly. Stir in the melted butter. Spoon into the prepared tin and press down evenly using the back of a spoon. Bake in the heated oven for 45 minutes. Cool in the tin and cut into 16 fingers.

Peanut Crunchies

Illustrated opposite

oil for greasing baking sheets
275 g /10 oz crunchy peanut butter
175 g /6 oz castor sugar · 1 egg

Set the oven at moderate 180 C, 350 F, gas 4, and grease 2 baking sheets. Put all the ingredients into a mixing bowl and beat well for 1 minute. Roll the mixture into 2·5 cm /1 in balls. Place well apart on the baking sheets, flatten slightly with the back of a fork and bake in the heated oven for about 15 to 20 minutes until golden brown. Transfer to a wire rack and leave to cool. Makes about 24 biscuits.

Clockwise from the back Cheesy Bunny (page 80), Rib-sticking Parkin and Peanut Crunchies (above), Mackerel Pâté (page 80) and Pain Perdu (page 88).

Lunch Boxes

Do you remember your school dinners? I certainly do, and not always with relish. A predictable dish was trotted out on each day of the week, and it was pretty dull fare. The puddings produced some fairly gory names: jam sponge was known as 'road accident', steamed suet roll was called 'dead baby'. Sorry, but children are quite insensitive when it comes to these things. I believe that meals have improved in a lot of schools where a canteen system has been set up, and there are several dishes and salads to choose from. Some schools, however, have stopped serving lunch altogether and children wander out to chip shops and snack bars. I think a well-prepared lunch box is a much better solution, and can be cheaper, more interesting, and every bit as nourishing if you use your imagination. It is a good idea to make it up the night before to save panic in the morning and store it in the fridge to keep the food fresh. Actually, there's no reason why the older and more capable children shouldn't be encouraged to make up their own lunch boxes. Another important thing is to have an attractive, suitably sized box with an airtight lid, one which holds plenty, but fits easily into a satchel. A plastic ice cream container is a good thought, or there are some lovely tin boxes around now – copies of old Oxo or toffee tins. However, the child is not going to eat the container, so let's think about what to put in it.

Of course, there's nothing wrong with the good old sandwich, as long as it has a nourishing filling and doesn't get soggy. Pâté, salami, liver sausage, mortadella, scrambled egg and crispy bacon are excellent as a change from cheese and ham. I like to put a salad in a separate small container so that it doesn't make the bread wet. I leave the tomatoes whole, slice up a raw carrot, or add a couple of sticks of celery to watercress or lettuce leaves. Salt in a twist of foil is a good idea for those who like it. Filled buns and baps are excellent for lunch boxes. So are cooked sausages, Cornish pasties, sausage rolls, Scotch eggs and chicken drumsticks. It's also a good idea to include a good crisp apple, pear, or a firm banana (over-ripe

From the top Stuffed Pitta Bread (page 96), School Cake (page 99) with a Crunchie and fudge yogurt milkshake, Cheese Crunchies (page 95) and Sardines in a Roll (page 98).

bananas go horribly black in a tin). Don't forget to include a paper napkin, and if you can run to it, older girls will appreciate a single sachet containing a cologne-soaked tissue for wiping sticky fingers, and freshening up on hot days. I always wrap sandwiches and baps in foil. It doesn't leak, and you can wipe it clean, and use the other side on the second day as an economy measure.

In cold weather, think about packing a small thermos of hot soup into the satchel. A hot starter makes a feast out of a cold lunch.

Lunch Box Ideas

Try to get your children interested in helping to put together their midday meal. With a little help and encouragement even the 'smalls' can learn to butter bread rolls, and choose a piece of fruit to go into the lunch box. Nowadays a hot lunch is easy – wide-necked thermos flasks come in (almost) child- and school-proof varieties, which can be used for chunky soups or casseroles (carefully reheated from the previous night's supper).

See the chapter on picnics for more ideas.

Store interesting buns, baps, rolls and bread in the freezer to cut down on shopping expeditions and always ensure fresh bread. These help ring the changes on the usual schooltime fare. Simply

defrost in the fridge overnight, and fill with any of the following, or your own favourite mixtures.

Marmite and slices of Cheddar cheese (or lettuce and Marmite).

Tinned sardines in tomato sauce, mashed, with a crisp lettuce leaf.

Hard boiled eggs, mashed with a little mayonnaise and mixed with a little diced tomato.

Chopped hard-boiled eggs mixed with cream cheese with chives.

Frankfurter Rolls (page 84).

Cheese Crunchies

Illustrated on page 92

50 g / 2 oz soft margarine
100 g / 4 oz Cheddar cheese, grated
50 g / 2 oz cornflakes, crushed
50 g / 2 oz wholewheat flour

Mix together all ingredients. Place walnut-sized balls onto baking trays, flattening them with the back of a fork. Bake at 180 C, 350 F, gas 4 for 10 to 15 minutes. Remove and cool on a rack. Makes 25.

Milkshakes

Transported to school in a thermos flask, ice cubes and ice cream will still be icy at lunchtime. Here are a few ideas to get you going.

In a blender / liquidiser whizz together:

1 strawberry yogurt, 150 ml / $\frac{1}{2}$ pint chilled milk, a few ice cubes
or a scoop or vanilla or strawberry ice cream

or

1 Crunchie bar (broken-up), 1 fudge yogurt, 150 ml / $\frac{1}{4}$ pint
chilled milk and a few ice cubes

or

1 banana, 300 ml / $\frac{1}{2}$ pint chilled milk, 1 scoop vanilla ice cream,
1 teaspoon brown sugar

or

300 ml / $\frac{1}{2}$ pint chilled milk, 1 tablespoon drinking chocolate
powder, 1 packet Maltesers (or a small bar whole nut chocolate)
and a few ice cubes

Stuffed Pitta Bread

FOR EACH SERVING
1 piece pitta bread (plain or wholemeal)
15 g / ½ oz butter or soft margarine
2 eggs, beaten with 2 tablespoons milk
50 g / 2 oz ham, cooked bacon, salami or cooked chicken, diced
25 g / 1 oz cheese, diced (optional)
salt and pepper to taste

Cut off the top of the pitta bread, and open out the bread to make a pocket.

Melt the butter in a small pan. Add the beaten egg mixture and cook gently, stirring, until the eggs are lightly scrambled. Stir in the remaining ingredients and season to taste. Spoon into the pitta bread. Replace the top and wrap in greaseproof paper or aluminium foil. This is equally good eaten hot or cold.

Pitta Bread Fillings

Apple and cheese filling

Mix together 1 apple, cored and chopped, 50 g / 2 oz cottage cheese, 1 tablespoon raisins, 1 stalk celery, chopped. Or substitute 50 g / 2 oz grated Cheddar cheese and 1 tablespoon mayonnaise for the cottage cheese.

Tuna filling

Illustrated on page 93

Mix together 2 tablespoons flaked canned tuna, 2 tablespoons yogurt and a few slices cucumber.

Chicken filling

Mix together 75 g / 3 oz diced cooked chicken or turkey, 2 tablespoons mayonnaise or yogurt, a little curry powder (optional) and a few raisins.

Egg and Bacon Butties

FOR EACH SERVING
1 bap
a little oil or lard for frying
1 egg
3 rashers back or streaky bacon

Cut the bap in half almost all the way through, leaving a 'hinge'. Heat the oil in a frying pan and lightly fry the egg. Drain on kitchen paper. Meanwhile, grill or fry the bacon until crispy and drain on kitchen paper. Place the bacon on the bottom half of the bap, folding the bacon if necessary. Place the egg on the bacon and top with the remaining half of the bun. Wrap in aluminium foil.

Cheese Puffs

1 (85-g/3-oz) sheet from a 340 g/12 oz packet frozen puff pastry
sheets, thawed
4 small 'Baby-bel' cheeses
4 thin slices ham
1 egg, beaten

Set the oven at 220 C, 425 F, gas 7. Roll out the pastry to a 20-cm/8-in square, 1·5 mm/$\frac{1}{16}$ in thick. Cut into 4 10-cm/4-in squares. Remove the red rind from cheeses. Cut the ham into squares, slightly smaller than the pastry squares. Brush the pastry lightly with beaten egg, and place a slice of ham on each square of pastry. Place a cheese on each, and fold the pastry in half to form a triangle. Press edges firmly to seal. Place the triangles on a baking sheet, and brush the tops with beaten egg. Bake in the heated oven for 15 to 20 minutes until puffed and golden brown. Serve warm or cold.

Sardines in a Roll

Illustrated on page 92

1 (85-g/3-oz) sheet puff pastry from a 340 g/12 oz pack frozen
puff pastry, thawed
1 (115-g/4-oz) can sardines in tomato sauce
1 egg, beaten (optional)

Set the oven at 220 C, 425 F, gas 7. Roll out the pastry
1·5 mm/$\frac{1}{16}$ in thick, to a rectangle 30 × 10 cm/12 × 4 in. Cut the
pastry into 4 strips each 7·5 × 10 cm/3 × 4 in. Open the can of
sardines, and divide them equally between the 4 strips, discarding
the sauce. Brush the edges with beaten egg. Roll up like a sausage
roll, sealing the edge firmly. Brush with beaten egg. Transfer to a
baking sheet. Bake in the heated oven for 7 to 10 minutes until
puffed and golden. Makes 4.

Grasmere Ginger Shortcake

100 g/4 oz wholemeal self-raising flour
100 g/4 oz soft light brown sugar
1 teaspoon ground ginger
100 g/4 oz fine oatmeal
100 g/4 oz butter, melted

Set the oven at 160 C, 325 F, gas 3, and grease and line the base of a
25 × 15 cm/10 × 6 in tin. Mix together the flour, sugar and ginger
and oatmeal in a mixing bowl. Stir in the butter until well mixed
but still crumbly. Using the back of a spoon, press the mixture into
the tin. Bake in the heated oven until golden brown for 20 to 25
minutes. Remove from the oven and immediately cut into 20
fingers. Allow to cool in the tin.

School Cake

Illustrated on page 92

100 g /4 oz butter
350 g /12 oz dried mixed fruit
2 teaspoons mixed spice
$\frac{1}{2}$ teaspoon bicarbonate of soda
200 g /7 oz demerara sugar
250 ml /8 fl oz boiling water
pinch of salt
250 g /9 oz wholemeal flour
2 eggs
1 teaspoon baking powder

Set the oven at moderate, 180 C, 350 F, gas 4. Grease and line a 20 cm /8 in round cake tin. Grease the greaseproof paper lining. Put the butter, fruit, mixed spice, bicarbonate of soda, sugar, boiling water and salt in a large saucepan. Bring to a boil, then simmer for 5 minutes. Remove from the heat, cool for 5 minutes then stir in the flour, eggs and baking powder.

Turn the mixture into the tin and bake in the heated oven for $1\frac{1}{4}$ hours or until a skewer, when inserted into the cake, comes out clean. Cool in the tin, then turn out and wrap in greaseproof paper or aluminium foil. Keep for a couple of days before serving.

Cowboy Cake

275 g / 10 oz plain flour
pinch of salt
275 g / 10 oz soft brown sugar
175 g / 6 oz butter or margarine
2 teaspoons baking powder
$\frac{1}{2}$ teaspoon bicarbonate of soda
1 teaspoon mixed spice
200 ml / 7 fl oz soured milk
2 eggs, beaten

Grease and line the bases of 2 20-cm / 8-in square cake tins. Set the oven at 190 C, 375 F, gas 5.

Sift the flour, salt and sugar into a mixing bowl. Rub in the butter or margarine until the mixture resembles coarse breadcrumbs. Measure 8 tablespoons of the mixture and set aside. Add the baking powder, bicarbonate and mixed spice to the remaining mixture in the bowl. Mix well. Stir in the milk and eggs and mix thoroughly. Divide the mixture between the prepared tins, cook for 5 minutes and then sprinkle over the reserved mixture. Bake in the heated oven for 25 to 30 minutes. Turn out carefully and cut into 32 5-cm / 2-in squares when cool.

Note. To make soured milk, add a few drops of lemon juice to fresh milk and warm very gently. For older children chopped nuts and cinnamon can be sprinkled over the top crumbly layer.

Apricot Bars

225 g / 8 oz soft margarine
225 g / 8 oz soft light brown sugar
1 egg yolk
275 g / 10 oz wholemeal flour
1 teaspoon baking powder
1 (115-g / 4-oz) packet chopped mixed nuts
1 (340-g / 12-oz) jar apricot jam or conserve
oil for greasing

Set the oven at moderate, 180 C, 350 F, gas 4, and grease a shallow 30 × 20 cm / 12 × 8 in baking dish or tin. Put the margarine, sugar, egg yolk, flour, baking powder and nuts into a mixing bowl. Beat for 1 minute until thoroughly mixed, then knead to form a soft but sticky dough. Put half the mixture into the tin and smooth into an even layer. Spread the jam over, then top with the remaining mixture, again patting it into an even layer.

Bake in the heated oven for 40 minutes until golden brown. Allow to cool in the tin, then cut into 16 bars.

Note. Any flavour jam can be used for this recipe and currants or sultanas used instead of nuts.

Best Ever Flapjack

100 g / 4 oz butter or margarine
4 tablespoons golden syrup
1 tablespoon soft dark brown sugar
1 tablespoon raisins
1 tablespoon chopped nuts
25 g / 1 oz chopped glacé cherries
1 tablespoon cocoa
225 g / 8 oz porridge oats

Set the oven at 180 C, 350 F, gas 4. Grease an 18-cm / 7-in square cake tin. Melt the butter with the syrup and sugar over a low heat, then remove from the heat and stir in the remaining ingredients. Press into the prepared tin and bake in the heated oven for 20 to 25 minutes. Cut into 14 fingers whilst still warm. When cool store in an airtight container.

Chocolate Biscuits

275 g / 10 oz soft margarine
150 g / 5 oz icing sugar
pinch of salt · 350 g / 12 oz plain flour
75 g / 3 oz cocoa · oil for greasing

Cream the margarine with the sugar until light and fluffy. Sift together the salt, flour and cocoa and mix into the butter mixture. Knead until smooth. Shape into a long roll 6 cm / $2\frac{1}{2}$ inches in diameter. Wrap in foil, greaseproof or cling film and chill in the freezer or refrigerator until firm.

Heat the oven to 190 C, 375 F, gas 5. Grease a baking tray. Cut the dough into slices 5 mm / $\frac{1}{4}$ in thick and bake on the prepared tray for 15 minutes. Cool on a wire rack.

Note. The mixture, once made, can be tightly wrapped and stored in the freezer (or for 3 days in a fridge). Just slice off as many biscuits as you need.

Parties

Giving a party need not be the terrifying ordeal it conjures up, because food for a children's party doesn't necessarily mean days of preparation and complicated baking. I found that the most successful birthday parties I gave for the boys were the simplest. To start with, children are not really interested in large creamy cakes (except for use as ammunition). They like savoury things – twiglets and crisps and frozen cocktail sausage rolls, freshly baked and still warm. They like processed cheese spread on small cheese crackers and savoury dips with lots of different things to dunk them in. To my surprise, I discovered that the majority of youngsters don't like jellies and blancmanges. They do, however, love ice cream, especially chocolate and strawberry.

A good rule to go by is 'small things for small mouths'. You will be rewarded with Oohs and Aahs of delight if you go in for novelty value and use your imagination to make the food look colourful and pretty. Cut thin bread into interesting shapes with buscuit cutters, and spread with red jam or lemon curd. Dot them with Smarties for eyes and buttons. You will intrigue children enormously by making things that pretend to be what they are not, like the panda cake and the Christmas tree cake included in these recipes. Make sure there are plenty of pleasant drinks available. Excited children get mighty thirsty. Use paper tablecloths, plates and beakers. No breakages and very little washing up.

BONFIRE PARTY FOR 8

Hamburgers with Relish · Texan Beans
Baked Potatoes · Walnut Pie and Ice Cream

Hamburgers with Relish

1 kg / 2 lb very lean minced beef
2 onions, chopped
1 egg, beaten
1 (285-g / 10-oz) jar tomato chutney
salt and pepper, to taste
8 hamburger buns, split
1 Iceberg lettuce, washed
TO SERVE
ketchup, mustard, tomato chutney, onion rings, mayonnaise,
cheese slices

To make the hamburgers, mix the beef with the chopped onions, egg, chutney and seasonings. Divide the mixture into 8, and shape into hamburgers. Chill until needed. Fry or grill the hamburgers, in batches, for about 3 to 4 minutes on each side, depending on thickness. Keep warm in the oven until ready. Let the guests 'build' their own burgers if they are old enough – by having a dish full of split burger buns next to the cooked burgers, and all the accompaniments. This way, each child can choose what goes into his or her hamburger.

Texan Beans

1 (840-g / 1·85-lb) can baked beans
1 (376-g / 13¼-oz) can barbecue flavour cook-in-sauce

Mix the beans and sauce together and heat gently until very hot.

Baked Potatoes

8 large baking potatoes, scrubbed
salt

Heat the oven to 190 C, 375 F, gas 5. Put the potatoes in a roasting tin and sprinkle with a little salt. Bake in the heated oven until soft – about 1 to 1½ hours, depending on size and type. Serve with various toppings:
1. Mix 225 g / 8 oz softened butter with 2 tablespoons Bovril or Marmite. Spoon into a bowl, or shape into a roll and wrap in foil, and chill until firm.

2. Mix 2 85-g / 2-3-oz packets cream cheese flavoured with chives and garlic herbs, with 142 ml / 5 fl oz soured cream.

Walnut Pie

Not as expensive as traditional Pecan Pie and just as wonderful.

1 (368-g / 13-oz) packet frozen shortcrust pastry, thawed
175 g / 6 oz soft margarine
175 g / 6 oz soft dark brown sugar
4 large or 5 medium eggs
250 g / 9 oz golden syrup
few drops vanilla essence
grated rind and juice of 1 lemon
350 g / 12 oz walnut halves

Set the oven at 180 C, 350 F, gas 4. Roll out the pastry to a rectangle 25 × 33 cm / 10 × 13 in. Use it to line a rectangular shallow roasting or baking tin, or deep Swiss roll tin 20 × 30 cm / 8 × 12 in. Prick well and bake blind in the heated oven for 15 minutes.
   Meanwhile, make the filling – beat the margarine and sugar until smooth and fluffy. Gradually beat in the eggs, warm the syrup and stir into the mixture with the remaining ingredients. Spoon into the pastry case and bake for about 40 to 50 minutes. Serve warm with ice cream.

BARBECUE PARTY FOR 8

Illustrated on page 109

Special Spare Ribs with Sticky Rice
Chef's Salad · Foil-baked Bananas
Summer Fruit Punch

Special Spare Ribs

The ribs take quite a while – about 1¼ hours – to cook on the barbecue but they're well worth waiting for; their taste is just out of this world.

2 kg/4½ lb pork spare ribs
1 teaspoon salt
a little oil
SAUCE
2 large onions, grated
3 tablespoons soft dark brown sugar
150 ml/¼ pint wine vinegar
300 ml/½ pint tomato ketchup
2 tablespoons soy sauce
2 tablespoons Worcestershire sauce
1 teaspoon mustard powder

Rub the meat with the salt. Brush the grill with a little oil to prevent the meat from sticking, then place the ribs onto the grill. The fire should be medium hot. Cook, turning every 10 minutes, for about 40 minutes.

For the sauce, which can be made ahead and kept in the fridge, mix all the ingredients together in a saucepan, then bring to a boil, stirring continuously, and simmer gently for 2 minutes. When the ribs have cooked for 40 minutes, brush them with the sauce and cook for a further 35 minutes, turning and brushing with sauce regularly to prevent the meat from burning. To serve, cut in between the ribs and spoon over any remaining sauce.

Sticky Rice

25 g / 1 oz butter
225 g / 8 oz streaky bacon, coarsely chopped
100 g / 4 oz button mushrooms
450 g / 1 lb long grain American rice
1 (425-g / 15-oz) can French onion soup
600 ml / 1 pint water · salt and pepper to taste

Heat the oven to 180 C, 350 F, gas 4. Melt the butter in a flameproof and ovenproof casserole. Add the bacon and fry until golden. Add the mushrooms and brown them quickly. Stir in the rice, cook for 1 minute then stir in the soup, the water and seasoning. Bring to a boil then cover and cook in the heated oven for 25 minutes, until all the liquid has been absorbed and the rice is tender.

Chef's Salad

1 Iceberg lettuce, torn up
1 head Chinese leaves, sliced
small bunch radishes, thinly sliced
1 (198-g / 7-oz) can sweet corn kernels, or baby corn
3 tomatoes, sliced · 8 spring onions
½ cucumber, diced · 50 g / 2 oz raisins
DRESSING
150 ml / ¼ pint sunflower seed oil
2 tablespoons wine vinegar
1 teaspoon mustard powder · salt and pepper to taste
1 tablespoon sesame seeds

Prepare all the salad ingredients in advance and wrap, separately, in cling film then chill until ready to serve the salad. Make the dressing by putting all the ingredients in a screw-top jar and shaking until well mixed. Put the lettuce and Chinese leaves in a large salad bowl. Add half the dressing and toss the salad well. Arrange the remaining ingredients separately on top of the salad in the bowl. Spoon over the remaining dressing and serve as soon as possible.

Foil-baked Bananas

8 bananas
2 (411-g / 14½-oz) cans apricot halves in apple juice
8 rectangles aluminium foil each 20 × 25 cm / 8 × 10 in
4 tablespoons chopped nuts
8 scoops vanilla ice cream

Slice the bananas in half lengthways. Drain the apricots and reserve the juice for the summer fruit punch. Purée the apricots by blending in a liquidiser or pushing through a sieve. Place each banana on a rectangle of foil so that the halves lie side by side, cut surface uppermost. Spoon the purée over the bananas, sprinkle with the nuts then fold the foil over the bananas. Twist the ends tightly and make sure the top seam is well sealed. Place on the barbecue grill and cook for 10 minutes.

To serve, place each package on a dessert plate and open carefully. Spoon vanilla ice cream into the foil packages and eat immediately.

Note. The bananas can also be baked in a moderate oven (180 C, 350 F, gas 4) for 20 minutes.

Summer Fruit Punch

225 g / ½ lb strawberries
1 litre / 1¾ pints orange juice
1 litre / 1¾ pints apple juice
1 litre / 1¾ pints grapefruit juice
1 litre / 1¾ pints lemonade

Make ice cubes in the usual way but first place a hulled strawberry in each one before freezing. Or place the strawberries in a ring mould, fill with water and freeze. Chill the juice and lemonade until ready to serve. Mix the juices and lemonade together in a big bowl. Decorate with the turned-out ice ring or the ice cubes.

A barbecue party f r 8 (pages 106-8). Special Spare Ribs with Sticky Rice, Chef's Salad, Foil-baked Bananas and Summer Fruit Punch.

Mammoth Party Dish

40 frankfurters, quartered, or sausages
6 tablespoons oil
4 tablespoons flour
3 (310-g/10·9-oz) jars Italian or Napoletana tomato sauce
2 (397-g/14-oz) cans chopped tomatoes
1·5 kg/3½ lb spaghetti or noodles
75 g/3 oz butter
salt and pepper to taste

Heat the oil in a frying pan and brown the sausages – about 5 minutes (there is no need to brown the frankfurters). Stir in the flour, followed by the tomato sauce and chopped tomatoes. Bring to a boil, stirring constantly. Add the frankfurters or sausages, lower the heat and simmer gently for 10 minutes. Meanwhile cook the spaghetti or noodles according to the directions on the packet. Drain when cooked and toss in the butter and a little salt and pepper to taste. Transfer the spaghetti or noodles to a warmed shallow serving dish and spoon the sauce and sausages on top. SERVES 20.

Tip: cook the spaghetti in batches.

Christmas Tree Cake (page 118), Marshmallow Delights (page 121), Chocolate-dipped Fruits and marzipan acorns (page 124).

Gingerbread People

250 g / 9 oz wholemeal flour
2 teaspoons ground ginger
½ teaspoon ground cinnamon
100 g / 4 oz butter or hard margarine
75 g / 3 oz soft brown sugar
4 tablespoons golden syrup
D E C O R A T I O N
a few currants, pieces of candied peel,
glacé cherries, white icing

Set the oven at moderate, 180 C, 350 F, gas 4. Sift the dry ingredients together into a mixing bowl. Rub in the butter or hard margarine until the mixture resembles coarse breadcrumbs. Stir in the sugar and the syrup. Knead the mixture until smooth. Roll out on a floured surface to 5 mm / ¼ in thick. Cut out gingerbread men and women, kneading the trimmings together and re-rolling so that all the dough is used.

Place the gingerbread people on greased baking trays. Decorate before baking, using icing to make hair, currants for eyes and buttons, candied peel for a nose, a slice of glacé cherry for lips. Bake in the heated oven for 8 to 10 minutes. Allow to cool slightly on the trays before transferring to wire racks. Makes about 10, depending on size.

Nanny's Pudding

1 kg / 2 lb mixed fresh or frozen soft fruits: choose from
raspberries, redcurrants, blackcurrants or loganberries
225 g / 8 oz castor sugar
10-12 slices bread, crusts removed
75 g / 3 oz butter, softened

Prepare your chosen fruit and put it into a saucepan with the castor
sugar. Stir gently to mix then cook together over a gentle heat for
not more than 5 minutes – just long enough to make the juices run.

Spread the sliced bread with softened butter and use them to line
the bottom and sides of a 1-litre / 1¾-pint pudding basin, putting
the buttered side next to the basin. Pour in the warm fruit, and top
the pudding with more sliced bread, this time with the buttered
side next to the fruit. Cover with a small plate that will fit inside the
basin and place weights on top. Leave overnight in the fridge, then
turn out – onto a shallow dish so that the juice won't overflow –
and serve with lashings of whipped or single cream. SERVES 4 to 6.

Harlequin in a Hurry

*Block or soft scoop ice cream and fresh or frozen fruit make instant and
extremely appealing party treats. Use any combination of colours and
flavours you fancy (although my children always insisted on including
chocolate and lemon) to make the harlequin as jolly as possible.*

1 litre / 1¾ pints ice cream
½ kg / 1 lb fresh, tinned or frozen fruit
300 ml / ½ pint whipped cream

Put slices from block ice cream in the bottom of a large dish, or
individual dishes, or spread a layer of soft scoop ice cream. Follow
with a layer of fruit (raspberries, peaches and bananas are always
well received). Build up different coloured layers until you have
filled your dish or dishes, finishing with fruit, and top with piped
whipped cream. Store in the freezer until needed. SERVES 8.

Great Aunt Ethel's Pudding

BASE
200 g / 7 oz Ritz crackers, crushed
225 g / 8 oz walnuts, chopped, or chopped mixed nuts
350 g / 12 oz castor sugar
1 teaspoon baking powder
few drops vanilla essence or coffee essence
100 g / 4 oz mixed dried fruit – sultanas, raisins, cherries
6 egg whites, stiffly beaten
TOPPING
300 ml / $\frac{1}{2}$ pint whipping cream
fruit – such as 225 g / $\frac{1}{2}$ lb strawberries or 2 bananas or a
small tin of mandarins, drained

Set the oven at 180 C, 350 F, gas 4. Grease two 23-cm / 9-in sandwich tins. Line the bases with greaseproof paper and grease again.

Put all the dry ingredients for the base in a bowl and mix thoroughly. Fold in the beaten egg whites. Spoon this mixture into the baking tins and spread evenly. Bake in the heated oven for 30 to 35 minutes until firm and dry. Cool. Whip the cream and prepare the fruit. Spread the cream onto the bases and decorate with fruit. SERVES 12 to 16.

Rock Cakes

225 g / 8 oz plain flour
2 teaspoons baking powder
¼ teaspoon ground mixed spice
75 g / 3 oz butter or hard margarine
75 g / 3 oz granulated sugar
25 g / 1 oz each currants, sultanas, raisins and chopped mixed peel
1 egg, beaten with 1 tablespoon milk

Set the oven at moderately hot, 200 C, 400 F, gas 6. Lightly grease 2 baking trays. Sift the flour, baking powder and spice into a mixing bowl. Add the butter or margarine, cut in small cubes, and rub in with your fingertips until the mixture resembles breadcrumbs. Stir in the sugar, dried fruit and peel. Stir in the beaten egg and milk; the resulting mixture should be stiff, the same consistency as dough. Put heaped teaspoonsful of the mixture on the baking sheet – they should have a rough and rocky texture.

Bake in the heated oven for 10 to 15 minutes or until firm and golden. Cool on a wire rack. Makes 20 rock cakes.

Note. These rock cakes are best eaten the same day, although stale ones are good split and buttered. They freeze well.

Coconut Pyramids

These were always a favourite at my sons' birthday parties. They are also very easy, and great fun, for them to make themselves. They are too simple to need a 'proper' recipe as such: just mix desiccated coconut into condensed milk until you have a mixture thick enough to shape. Put into separate bowls and colour each batch differently – if you wish. Then line a baking tray with rice paper and shape the mixture into little pyramid shapes on it. Bake in a moderate oven (180 C, 350 F, gas 4) for about 15 minutes. Top each with a glacé cherry for the party.

Panda Cake

FOR THE VANILLA SPONGE CAKE
100 g / 4 oz self-raising flour · 1 teaspoon baking powder
pinch of salt · 100 g / 4 oz castor sugar
2 large eggs · 100 g / 4 oz soft margarine
a few drops vanilla essence

(or you can use a packet of vanilla sponge cake mix to make the cake)

FOR THE CHOCOLATE SPONGE CAKE
75 g / 3 oz self-raising flour · 25 g / 1 oz cocoa powder
1 teaspoon baking powder · pinch of salt
100 g / 4 oz castor sugar
100 g / 4 oz soft margarine · 2 large eggs

(or you can use a packet of chocolate sponge cake mix to make the cake)

FOR THE ICING
100 g / 4 oz butter · 6 tablespoons milk
575 g / 1¼ lb icing sugar

DECORATION
chocolate buttons · 2 mini Swiss rolls
2 tablespoons cocoa powder

Set the oven at 180 C, 350 F, gas 4. Grease and line the base of a
20-cm / 8-in round sandwich tin, and an 18-cm / 7-in square cake tin.
First make the vanilla sponge. Sift the flour, baking powder and
salt into a mixing bowl. Add the sugar, the eggs and the margarine,
cut into small pieces. Using an electric whisk or a wooden spoon,
stir until all the ingredients are mixed, then beat at high speed for 1
minute until the mixture is very smooth. Beat in the vanilla. Spoon
the mixture into the prepared round sandwich tin, and bake in the
heated oven for 15 to 20 minutes, or until a cocktail stick or skewer
inserted in the centre comes out clean. Turn out onto a wire rack to
cool. Or, if using a packet sponge cake, mix and make according to
the directions on the packet.
For the chocolate sponge cake, follow the method for the vanilla
sponge, sifting the cocoa with the flour. Bake the mixture in the
prepared square tin for 15 to 20 minutes in the heated oven. Again,

if using chocolate sponge cake mix, follow the directions on the packet.

To make the icing, place all the ingredients in a basin over a saucepan of hot water. Stir until the butter has melted. Remove from the heat and leave to cool. Beat well until thick and smooth. Divide the mixture in two. Add 2 tablespoons of cocoa powder to one half and beat well.

To assemble the cake, cut the corners off the chocolate cake (see diagram) and use these trimmings to make 2 ears and 2 paws. The round chocolate cake will form the head. The vanilla cake will form the body.

To make up the panda, place the cakes on a large tray and cover the head with white icing. Cover the body with brown icing and put next to the head. Cover the ears and paws with brown icing and stick onto the outer edges of the cake with a little left-over icing. Cut the Swiss rolls in half. Cover with brown icing. Stick two halves onto the head to form eyes, and the other two on the body to form the front paws. Decorate each eye with a blob of white icing and a chocolate drop. Put the remainder of the white icing in a piping bag fitted with a small plain tube and pipe eyelashes, and toes, nose and mouth if wished. SERVES 12 to 16.

Christmas Tree Cake

Illustrated on page 110

CAKE
250 g / 9 oz soft margarine
250 g / 9 oz castor sugar
3 eggs, beaten
175 g / 6 oz golden syrup
75 g / 3 oz ground almonds
250 g / 9 oz self-raising flour
75 g / 3 oz cocoa
$\frac{1}{4}$ teaspoon each salt and baking powder
275 ml / 9 fl oz milk

ICING
200 g / 7 oz butter
200 g / 7 oz cream cheese
350 g / 12 oz icing sugar

FOR DECORATING
9 cake candles and candle holders
sugar strands
chocolate vermicelli
8 lengths red ribbon
8 small presents
cake board or tray

Set the oven at 180 C, 350 F, gas 4. Grease and line the base of a 23 × 33 cm / 9 × 13 in cake tin. Put the margarine, sugar, eggs, syrup and almonds into a mixing bowl. Sift the flour with the cocoa, salt and baking powder, and add with the milk. Beat all the ingredients together with a wooden spoon or electric beater until very smooth. Spoon into a cake tin and bake for 30 to 35 minutes, or until a cocktail stick or skewer comes out clean. Turn onto a wire rack to cool. Using a sharp knife, cut a Christmas tree shape from the cake (see photograph).

Next, make the icing. Cream the butter and cream cheese until smooth. Gradually beat in the icing sugar. Beat until light and fluffy. Put the cake on the platter, board or tray you intend to serve it from, and cover with the icing. Fork the icing to give the effect of branches. Use the spare cake to make the tree trunk. Sprinkle with sugar strands and chocolate vermicelli (see photograph). Attach one end of each piece of ribbon to the spike of a candle holder and push a candle holder (with ribbon attached) to the end of each branch. The remaining candle holder (without ribbon attached) goes on the top of the tree. (If you prefer, you can use a star or fairy for the top of the tree.) Place a candle in each holder. Using double-sided sticky tape or glue attach a present to the end of each piece of ribbon. It is quite a good idea to put a large name tag on each gift to avoid squabbles. Keep the cake in a cool place until ready to serve. SERVES 8 to 10.

Variation

To make Devil's Food Cake, follow the recipe for the cake above, but baking it in two greased and base-lined 23-cm/9-in sandwich tins. Make the icing as above and use to sandwich the cakes together and to coat the sides and top.

Fort Cake

1 18-cm/7-in square chocolate cake (follow the recipe for
chocolate sponge in Panda Cake on page 116)

ICING
50 g/2 oz softened butter or margarine
225 g/8 oz icing sugar, sieved
1 tablespoon cocoa powder
2 tablespoons milk

TO DECORATE
1 packet chocolate fingers or long orange-flavoured
chocolate sticks
toasted desiccated coconut (optional)
small plastic toy soldiers
small paper flag (the type used for sandcastles)
cake stand or tray

Stand the cake on the cake stand or tray. Make the icing by beating
the butter till smooth, then stirring in the icing sugar, cocoa and
milk. Beat until smooth and light.

Spread the icing thinly on the sides and top of the cake. Stick
chocolate fingers vertically around the sides of the cake to resemble
the outside of a fort. The fingers should be taller than the cake.
Place the toy soldiers around the edge of the inside of the fort, and
stick the flag in the centre of the cake. Sprinkle the coconut around
the base of the cake to resemble sand. SERVES 8 to 10.

Note. Toy cowboys and Indians on horseback can be placed
around the outside of the fort if space permits.

Marshmallow Delights

Illustrated on page 110

2 packets strawberry jelly
225 g / ½ lb frozen strawberries
3 teaspoons powdered gelatine
150 ml / ¼ pint cold water
150 ml / ¼ pint boiling water
150 g / 5 oz castor sugar
1 egg, separated
few drops vanilla essence

Make up the jellies according to the directions on the packet. Allow to cool to lukewarm. Divide the frozen strawberries between 10 tumblers or sundae glasses and pour the jelly over them to half-fill the glasses. Chill in the fridge until set. Sprinkle the gelatine over the cold water and leave until spongy – about 5 minutes. Add the boiling water and stir to dissolve. Transfer the mixture to a large mixing bowl. Add the sugar and the egg white to the just-warm gelatine mixture. Beat with an electric whisk until very thick and fluffy.

Beat in the egg yolk and vanilla very quickly then spoon on top of the jelly in the glasses and leave to set. If liked, decorate each glass with a strawberry. SERVES 10.

Variation

Use a can of drained mandarins in place of the strawberries, and replace 175 ml / 6 fl oz of the boiling water needed to make up the jellies with a 170-ml / 6 fl oz carton frozen, concentrated orange juice.

Number cakes

Use home-made or bought sponge cakes, any flavour, to cut out the numbers as shown. The cut out cakes can then be left plain or iced with any of the icings given in this book (see Orange Cake, Christmas Tree Cake and Panda Cake). Left-over pieces of cake (the shaded areas in the diagrams) can be used for making trifle, or in lunch boxes. Stick the cut out sponge shapes together with whichever icing you like, or jam.

One Use an 18-cm/7-in square sponge cake. Cut it in half to make 2 rectangles. Cut one of the rectangles in half again to make 2 squares. Cut 1 square in half to make 2 triangles. Assemble as shown.

Two Use 1 20-cm/8-in round sponge cake and either a 15-cm/6-in Swiss roll split in half lengthways *or* a 15-cm/6-in square cake halved to make a rectangle 15 × 7·5 cm/6 × 3 in. Assemble as shown.

Three Use 2 round 18-cm/7-in diameter sponge cakes. Take out the centre of each cake with a 5-cm/2-in biscuit cutter, then cut out a quarter of each cake. Assemble as shown.

Four Use 1 20-cm/8-in square sponge cake and 1 15-cm/6-in square sponge cake. Cut the larger cake in half to make 2

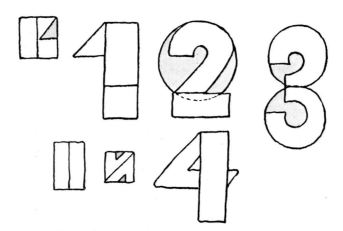

rectangles. Sandwich together with icing or jam to make a rectangle $20 \times 10\,\text{cm}/8 \times 4\,\text{in}$. Cut the smaller sponge in half diagonally to make 2 triangles. Cut a small triangle from the centre, then sandwich together. Assemble as shown.

Five Use an 18-cm/7-in square and an 18-cm/7-in round sponge cake. From the square sponge cut out a rectangle $8 \cdot 5 \times 10\,\text{cm}/3\frac{1}{2} \times 4\,\text{in}$. From this rectangle cut out an 8·5-cm/3-in square. Cut the round sponge as for the number 3. Assemble as shown.

Six Use 2 20-cm/8-in diameter round sponge cakes, and 1 15-cm/6-in square sponge. Cut a circle $7 \cdot 5\,\text{cm}/3\,\text{in}$ from the centre of each round sponge. Sandwich the two round sponges together. Cut the square cake in half and sandwich together to make a rectangle. Trim the ends of the rectangle to make the top stroke of the figure. Assemble as shown.

Seven Use 1 $33 \times 23\,\text{cm}/13 \times 9\,\text{in}$ sponge cake, baked in a Swiss roll tin. Cut and assemble as shown.

Eight Use 2 18-cm/7-in diameter round sponge cakes. Cut a 6-cm/$2\frac{1}{2}$-in circle from the centre of each and place one sponge above the other.

Nine Follow the method for 6.

Chocolate Biscuit Cake

225 g / 8 oz plain dessert chocolate, or Kake Brand
225 g / 8 oz butter
2 eggs
75 g / 3 oz castor sugar
225 g / 8 oz petit beurre or rich tea biscuits, roughly crushed
50 g / 2 oz glacé cherries, halved (optional)
50 g / 2 oz walnut halves (optional)

Melt the chocolate and butter together in a bowl set over a pan of hot (not simmering) water. Beat the sugar and eggs together until they are pale yellow in colour and form a ribbon when dropped from the whisk or electric beater. Beat in the chocolate mixture and fold in the biscuits (and the cherries and walnuts, if using).

Line a 15-cm / 6-in cake tin with greaseproof paper, spoon in the mixture and put it in the refrigerator to chill until firm, or until required. Serve turned out just as it is, or, for a richer, more celebratory cake, spread or pipe over in a decorative pattern with whipped cream. Serves 8.

Chocolate-dipped Fruits

Illustrated on page 110

Plain dessert or Kake Brand chocolate also make lovely little petit fours – child's play to make, a treat for them *and* for parents who come to collect at the end of the party.

To make these sweets, start by melting the chocolate in a bowl over a pan of hot water, then stir it till smooth. Have ready a selection of small fruits: I like dates, glacé cherries and mandarin segments, and strawberries are particularly good too. You can also use fondant mints and pieces of marzipan rolled into balls or shaped into acorns. As you dip each fruit or sweet thing lay it on a baking paper lined tray until the chocolate coating as set. Then put them into paper petits fours cases or arrange on small dishes.

Picnics

Picnickers are an astonishing breed. The weather may be unpredictable, and yet we still love to pack up a meal and eat outside. However inclement it might be, families can be seen lighting primus stoves, rigging up awnings and wind breaks, and often in the most unexpected places, like car parks or even by the sides of main arterial roads.

Some of the best picnics I ever went on took place in terrible weather, but I enjoyed the perversity of eating a cold egg sandwich in the pouring rain. There was such an air of hilarity about the whole proceedings . . . the sheer absurdity of it. Besides, there's something about eating outside that makes everything, even the most blackened, fire-roasted potato taste delicious.

The words 'Come on, let's go for a picnic' will raise the spirits of the most morose child, and now that we have the benefit of hot and cold insulated boxes, flasks and bags, it doesn't just have to be a picnic tea. Make a day of it, take lunch as well and, who knows, the sun might shine and then everything will be truly perfect.

Goloshes Soup

Illustrated on page 128

A cheery, spicy soup that will warm you right down to your gumboots, ideal for the day when you are in the mood for picnicking – but the weather isn't.

2 tablespoons oil
1 large onion, finely chopped
1 teaspoon paprika, or to taste
1 clove garlic, crushed (optional)
225 g / 8 oz potatoes, peeled and cut in small dice
1 red pepper, cut in small dice
1 (397-g / 14-oz) can chopped tomatoes
1 (425-g / 15-oz) can minced beef in gravy with onions
600 ml / 1 pint water or stock
salt and pepper to taste

Heat the oil in a saucepan. Add the onion and cook gently until very soft. Stir in the paprika and fry for 1 minute, then add the garlic, potatoes and pepper and fry, stirring constantly, for another minute. Add the tomatoes, mince and water or stock, stir, bring to a boil then simmer gently for 15 to 20 minutes until the potatoes are tender. Add a little salt and pepper to taste. Spoon into a warmed, wide-necked thermos flask, and serve with crusty bread rolls. SERVES 4.

A tip: if you are picnicking on a cold day and want something hot and filling, take a thermos of boiling water and some snack pots or pot rice to augment your cold hamper. Very cheering on a bleak outing.

Picnic Roulade (page 133) with a Tomato Hedgehog (page 137), Bow Tie Salad (page 135) and Quick Chocolate Cheesecake (page 140).

Thick Chicken Soup

2 chicken portions · 2 large onions
600 ml / 1 pint chicken stock (or a stock cube and water)
25 g / 1 oz rice
150 ml / $\frac{1}{4}$ pint single cream or milk
50 g / 2 oz frozen peas, thawed
salt and pepper to taste

Put the chicken, onions, rice and stock into a pan. Cover and bring to a boil. Simmer for 30 minutes or until the chicken is very tender. Remove the chicken from the liquid. When cool enough to handle, remove the skin and bones and any gristle and discard them. Roughly chop the chicken and place in a blender or processor with the liquid and vegetables from the pan. You will probably have to do it in a couple of batches. Blend until smooth and return to the pan with the cream or milk and peas. Add salt and pepper to taste and gently reheat. Pour into a warmed thermos flask. SERVES 4.

Quick Cheese Dip

350 g / 12 oz cream cheese
1 (298-g / 10$\frac{1}{2}$-oz) can consommé soup
TO SERVE
a selection of biscuits, crackers, crusty bread, raw carrots, celery, cucumber cut into sticks, radishes

Whisk the cheese with the cold soup until smooth, using a rotary or electric whisk, or in a blender. Pour into a suitable container and chill until firm.

Serve with lots of raw vegetables to dip in, or eat spread on bread, toast, or crackers. SERVES 4 to 6.

Orange Cake (page 142), Goloshes Soup (page 126), Wholemeal Sausage and Tomato Pie (page 134) with Quick Carrot Salad (page 136) and Hot Herby Bread (page 138).

Red Devil Soup

2 tablespoons oil
1 large onion, sliced
2 red peppers, chopped
2 (397-g/14-oz) cans chopped tomatoes
2 tablespoons tomato purée
300 ml/$\frac{1}{2}$ pint water or stock
salt and pepper to taste
pinch of sugar

Heat the oil in a saucepan, add the onion and cook gently until the onion is soft. Add the peppers and fry over medium heat for 2 to 3 minutes then stir in the remaining ingredients. Bring to a boil then cover and simmer for 15 minutes. Liquidise the mixture in a blender or processor or push through a sieve or food mill. Return to the pan and taste for seasoning. Add sugar. Reheat then pour into a warmed thermos flask. SERVES 4.

Egg and Bacon Quiche

PASTRY
175 g / 6 oz plain flour
pinch of salt
50 g / 2 oz butter or margarine
25 g / 1 oz lard or vegetable cooking fat
water to mix
FILLING
25 g / 1 oz butter or margarine
1 large onion, sliced
100 g / 4 oz streaky bacon, chopped
3 eggs, beaten
300 ml / $\frac{1}{2}$ pint milk
salt and pepper to taste

Set the oven at 180 C, 350 F, gas 4.

First make the pastry: sift the flour and salt into a mixing bowl. Cut the fats into small cubes and rub into the flour using your fingertips until the mixture resembles breadcrumbs. Gradually stir in enough cold water to make a soft but not sticky dough. Turn out onto a floured work surface and knead lightly until smooth. Using a well-floured rolling pin, roll the pastry out to a 25-cm / 10-in circle, and use to line a 20-cm / 8-in flan case. Prick the base and chill whilst preparing the filling.

Melt the butter in a frying pan, add the onions and cook gently until soft. Add the bacon and cook over medium high heat until the onions and bacon are golden brown. Cool. Beat the eggs with the milk and a little salt and pepper – be careful as the bacon may be salty. Spoon the onion and bacon mixture into the base of the flan case. Pour the egg mixture over. Carefully transfer to the heated oven and bake for 25 to 30 minutes until golden and set. Cut into wedges to serve. SERVES 4 to 6.

Variation

Beat 100 g / 4 oz grated cheese into the egg and milk mixture and follow the recipe above.

Portable Chicken and Ham Mayonnaise

half a cooked chicken
100 g / 4 oz sliced ham
1 (213-g / 7½-oz) can whole button mushrooms
1 (250-g / 9-oz) jar mayonnaise
1 (150-g / 5·28-oz) carton thick set whole milk natural yogurt
1 teaspoon curry powder, or to taste

Cut the chicken into small chunks, discarding the skin and bones.
Cut the ham into strips, and drain the mushrooms (or use 50 g / 2 oz
fresh mushrooms, washed and quartered). Mix the mayonnaise
with the yogurt and curry powder to taste and fold in the chicken,
ham and mushrooms. Serve with a rice or pasta salad. SERVES 4.

Rice and Easy
(or Twice as Rice)

175 g / 6 oz rice, cooked
1 (198-g / 7-oz) can sweet corn with peppers, drained
110 g / 4 oz packet frozen peas, cooked
100 g / 4 oz frozen prawns, thawed
6 tablespoons sunflower oil
2 tablespoons wine vinegar
salt and pepper to taste
½ teaspoon made mustard

Mix the cold, cooked rice with the sweet corn, cold cooked peas
and prawns. Mix the oil, vinegar, salt, pepper and mustard
together and then stir into the rice mixture until thoroughly
blended. Pack in a plastic box and chill before setting out, if
possible. SERVES 6.

Picnic Roulade

Illustrated on page 127

150 ml / ¼ pint soured cream
4 eggs, separated
100 g / 4 oz Cheddar cheese, grated
50 g / 2 oz fresh white breadcrumbs
salt and pepper to taste
3 tablespoons milk
FILLING
225 g / 8 oz frozen prawns, thawed
150 ml / ¼ pint mayonnaise
tomato ketchup
salt and pepper
¼ Iceberg lettuce

Set the oven at 200 C, 400 F, gas 6. Grease and line a
33 × 23 cm / 13 × 9 in Swiss roll tin with greased greaseproof paper.
Mix the soured cream with the egg yolks. Stir in the cheese,
breadcrumbs, seasonings and milk. Stiffly whisk the egg whites
with a pinch of salt and gently fold into the mixture using a large
metal spoon. Pour into the prepared tin and bake in the heated
oven for about 10 minutes, until firm and golden. Cover with a
clean damp tea towel and allow to cool.

Meanwhile, prepare the filling. Mix the frozen prawns with the
mayonnaise, a little tomato ketchup to taste and a pinch of salt and
pepper. Tear the lettuce leaves into pieces. Turn the roulade out
onto a piece of greaseproof paper. Spread with the prawn mixture
then cover with a layer of lettuce. Using the greaseproof paper,
loosely roll up the roulade like a Swiss roll. Transport in a
rectangular plastic food container. Do not chill. Serve at room
temperature, cut into thick slices. SERVES 4 to 6.

Wholemeal Sausage and Tomato Pie

Illustrated on page 128

PASTRY
275 g / 10 oz wholemeal flour
pinch of salt
65 g / 2½ oz lard
65 g / 2½ oz butter or hard margarine
75 g / 3 oz grated Cheddar cheese
2 to 3 tablespoons water to mix
FILLING
450 g / 1 lb sausagemeat
4 tomatoes
1 egg, beaten, to glaze

Set the oven at moderately hot, 190 C, 375 F, gas 5.

First, make the pastry. Mix the flour and salt in a mixing bowl. Add the lard and butter or margarine cut up into small pieces. Rub the fat into the flour with your fingertips until the mixture resembles coarse breadcrumbs. Stir in the grated cheese and enough water to make a soft but not sticky dough. Wrap the dough in greaseproof paper or cling film and leave to chill in the fridge while preparing the filling.

For the filling, mash the sausagemeat until smooth. Skin the tomatoes by immersing in boiling water for 7 seconds. The skins should then peel off easily. Quarter the tomatoes and remove the seeds. Coarsely chop the tomatoes and mix into the sausagemeat. Roll out a third of the pastry on a floured table, to make a 25-cm / 10-in circle. Use this circle to line a 25-cm / 10-in ovenproof pie plate. Roll out the remaining pastry to make a 30-cm / 12-in circle. Spoon the sausage and tomato filling onto the pastry base, leaving a 2·5-cm / 1-in border around the edge. Brush the pastry border with beaten egg and cover the pie with the pastry lid. Press the edges down well to seal, and make a slit in the centre to let out the steam. Brush the top with beaten egg and bake in the heated oven for 35 minutes, reducing the heat when you have put in the pie to 180 C, 350 F, gas 4. SERVES 6.

Bow Tie Salad

Illustrated on page 127

225 g / 8 oz pasta bows or spirals
4 tablespoons sunflower oil
1 tablespoon lemon juice
large pinch dry mustard
salt and pepper to taste
1 tablespoon snipped chives
50 g / 2 oz thinly sliced salami
100 g / 4 oz radishes

Cook the pasta in boiling salted water according to the directions on the packet. Drain and rinse thoroughly with hot water, then drain again well. Mix the oil with the lemon juice, mustard, salt, pepper and chives. Put the warm pasta in a mixing bowl and toss with the oil and lemon dressing. While the pasta cools, cut the salami into strips and slice the radishes. Stir into the pasta. Spoon into a plastic box for transporting to the picnic. SERVES 4 to 6.

Variation

Add a clove or two of crushed garlic to the oil and lemon juice dressing. For a more substantial salad, drain and flake a 225 g / 8 oz can of tuna fish, and add a few cooked green beans. Or slice a few cold, cooked sausages or frankfurters and mix into the salad.

Waldorf's Coleslaw

225 g / 8 oz white cabbage, grated or shredded
2 Granny Smith apples, cored and diced
4 stalks celery, sliced
50 g / 2 oz chopped walnuts (optional)
50 g / 2 oz raisins
1 (250-g / 9-oz) jar mayonnaise
salt and pepper to taste

Mix all the ingredients together until thoroughly blended. Spoon into a plastic box and chill well. SERVES 4.

Variation

Add a couple of grated raw carrots.

Quick Carrot Salad

Illustrated on page 128

450 g / 1 lb large carrots, peeled
4 tablespoons orange juice
1 tablespoon sunflower oil
salt and pepper to taste
1 tablespoon raisins (optional)
1 tablespoon sesame seeds

Grate the carrots. Mix the orange juice with the oil and season to taste. Toss the carrots with the orange juice mixture and stir in the raisins, if using. Spoon into a plastic picnic box and sprinkle with sesame seeds. Chill well before setting out. SERVES 4.

Tomato Hedgehogs

Illustrated on page 127

4 large tomatoes
3 hard-boiled eggs or $\frac{1}{2}$ cucumber
3 tablespoons sunflower oil
1 tablespoon wine vinegar
salt, pepper and mustard to taste

Turn each tomato onto its side and make cuts 5 mm / $\frac{1}{4}$ in apart, as if thinly slicing, but leave the slices joined at the base (don't cut all the way through).

If using hard-boiled eggs, slice with an egg-slicer. Slice the cucumber thinly.

Place a slice of cucumber or egg in each slit between the slices of tomato so the cucumber or egg sticks up above the tomato and forms spines. Mix the oil and vinegar together with a little salt, pepper and mustard to taste. Spoon over the tomatoes and arrange in a serving dish. Chill before serving. Plastic lidded boxes are ideal for transporting these, and any other salads. SERVES 4.

Hot Herby Bread

Illustrated on page 128

1 large French stick
175 g / 6 oz butter, softened
2 tablespoons chopped fresh herbs, a mixture of parsley, chives,
thyme, rosemary
2 to 3 cloves garlic, crushed (optional)

Set the oven at 180 C, 350 F, gas 4.

Cut the bread crossways in slices 1 cm / $\frac{1}{2}$ in thick, almost to the base. Blend the butter with the herbs and garlic, if using. Spread each slice with lashings of butter mixture. Wrap the loaf in foil and place on a baking sheet. Heat in the oven for 10 to 15 minutes until hot through. Wrap in newspaper then pop into an insulated 'hot' bag.* To serve, unwrap, and pull the slices apart.

Variation

Replace the butter with cream cheese. There is no need to heat in the oven.

*Insulated picnic bags can be used for keeping food either hot or cold. Baked potatoes wrapped in foil keep hot for ages in a well insulated bag, as do sausages and pies. Using frozen commercial 'ice-packs' in an insulated bag I've kept ice cream and cold mousses well chilled for several hours.

Remember, when you go picnicking, always take a box of wet-wipes, or a face cloth and a small towel. You and your children are bound to get sticky and grubby, and it's unlikely there'll be a hand basin in the middle of a field. And please encourage the family to take home every bit of litter. I live in a country area and am constantly appalled at the litter left behind by picnickers. It is not only very dangerous for animals to eat plastic and paper bags, but it also spoils the beauty of the countryside for others.

Baked Cheesecake

50 g / 2 oz soft margarine or butter
100 g / 4 oz castor sugar
275 g / 10 oz cottage cheese
2 eggs, separated
75 g / 3 oz ground almonds
grated rind and juice of 1 lemon
50 g / 2 oz raisins
icing sugar for dusting

Set the oven at 180 C, 350 F, gas 4. Grease and line the base of a 20-cm / 8-in shallow cake tin.

Place the margarine (or butter), sugar, and cheese in a mixing bowl and beat until smooth, using an electric beater or whisk if possible. Beat in the egg yolks, almonds and lemon rind and juice. Whisk the egg whites until they stand in stiff peaks and fold into the mixture with the raisins. Spoon into the prepared tin and bake in the heated oven until firm and golden brown – about 45 minutes. Cool in the tin and either serve, chilled, from the tin, or turn out onto a serving plate and chill before serving. Either way, dust with icing sugar, and serve with fresh fruit – raspberries are wonderful with this Hungarian cheesecake. SERVES 6.

Quick Chocolate Cheesecake

Illustrated on page 127

BASE
75 g / 3 oz cornflakes, crushed
50 g / 2 oz castor sugar
50 g / 2 oz butter, melted

FILLING
half a 127-g / 4½-oz lemon-flavoured block jelly
150 ml / ¼ pint boiling water
225 g / 8 oz cream cheese
50 g / 2 oz castor sugar
2 eggs, separated
100 g / 4 oz plain chocolate, melted

DECORATION
packet of chocolate buttons

Mix all the ingredients for the base together and then press onto the base of a 20-cm / 8-in flan case or cake tin.

Make up the jelly using the boiling water and chill until it thickens and is beginning to set (but it must still be liquid). Beat the cream cheese with the sugar, egg yolks and melted chocolate. Whisk the egg whites until stiff. Fold the jelly into the chocolate mixture, followed by the egg whites. Spoon on top of the base and leave to set in the refrigerator. Decorate with chocolate buttons. For easy transportation, put the cheesecake, in its flan case or cake tin, into a biscuit tin or large plastic box. SERVES 6 to 8.

Clafoutis

*This dish is as traditional to France as Yorkshire pudding is to
England. In fact, clafoutis is just a sweet version of Yorkshire pudding,
with fruit, such as prunes, cherries, plums, blackberries or apricots
added. Very good served hot or cold, with custard, ice cream or cream, it
makes a substantial rib-sticking end to a spring or autumn picnic.*

75 g / 3 oz plain flour
pinch of salt
50 g / 2 oz castor sugar
3 eggs, beaten
300 ml / $\frac{1}{2}$ pint milk
150 ml / $\frac{1}{4}$ pint single cream or top of the milk
1 (425-g / 15-oz) can stoneless black cherries or 227-g / 8-oz
packet frozen black cherries
50 g / 2 oz butter
icing sugar to dust

Set the oven at 200 C, 400 F, gas 6. Sift the flour, salt and sugar into
a mixing bowl. Add the eggs, milk and cream and beat to a smooth
batter. Drain the canned cherries (the juice is good in fruit salads,
or over ice cream or in jelly). Use half the butter to grease a large
ovenproof baking dish (such as a gratin dish). Spoon the cherries
into the dish and pour the batter over. Dot with remaining butter
and bake in the heated oven for 30 minutes until golden and firm.
Dust with icing sugar. SERVES 6.

Orange Cake

Illustrated on page 128

175 g / 6 oz soft margarine
175 g / 6 oz castor sugar
3 eggs, separated
175 g / 6 oz self-raising flour
½ teaspoon baking powder
grated rind and juice of 1 orange
3 tablespoons marmalade (not 'thick-cut')

ICING
100 g / 4 oz icing sugar
juice of ½ orange

Set the oven at 180 C, 350 F, gas 4. Grease and line the base of a
20-cm / 8-in deep cake tin.

Using an electric whisk or mixer, beat the margarine, castor
sugar and egg yolks together until light and fluffy. Beat in a quarter
of the flour, sifted with the baking powder, and the orange rind
and juice. Whisk the egg whites until stiff and fold into the mixture,
using a metal spoon, with the remaining flour. Spoon into the
prepared tin and bake in the heated oven until a cocktail stick or
skewer inserted into the centre comes out clean – about 40
minutes. Turn out and while still warm brush or spread with the
marmalade. Leave to cool. Mix the icing sugar with enough orange
juice to make a thick icing, and pour over the cake. Leave to set.

Index